Making Your Clothes FIT

A Step-by-Step Guide to Custom Fitting Home-Sewn and Ready-to-Wear Clothing

Patricia Burkhart Smith

Making Your Clothes FIT

DOLPHIN BOOKS

Doubleday & Co., Inc.   Garden City, N.Y.

1979

Library of Congress Cataloging in Publication Data
Smith, Patricia Burkhart.
Making Clothes Fit
Includes index.
1. Clothing and dress—Alteration. I. Title.
TT550.S64   646.4'3'04

ISBN: 0-385-14666-3
Library of Congress Catalog Card Number 78-20099

Contents

Introduction

Wrinkles and sags in clothing occur for two reasons: not enough material in the right place, which causes wrinkles, or too much material in the wrong place, which causes sags. The purpose of this book is to show you how, as quickly and easily as possible, to correct those wrinkles and sags that detract so much from the appearance of even expensive ready-made clothing, and scream "homemade" on garments made from commercially available patterns.

A well-fitting garment is a comfortable garment, because it can be put on and then forgotten. We've all experienced the discomfort of wearing an outfit for a special occasion which turned out to be more frustrating than special, because we spent the evening tugging and pulling on our garment, or running to the ladies' room to rearrange ourselves. If you go to your closet and pick out your favorite garment, you'll probably find that it's your best-fitting and most comfortable garment also. Unconsciously, we tend to choose clothing that not only enhances our appearance, but also makes us feel good. Only a well-fitted garment can do both.

Very few women come so close to having an average figure that they escape fitting problems entirely. A size 12 from one clothing manufacturer may fit you very differently than a size 12 from another company. It may not fit you at all. I have garments ranging from size 10 to size 16 in my closet that all fit me reasonably well.

These differences in size occur for many reasons. The federal government issues new "standard" measurements for all size ranges every few years. Clothing manufacturers may choose to follow any given set of these "standards," or they may develop measurements of their own. A change in the woman or girl used for the designers' fitting model can also produce changes in garment fit over a period of time.

Size differences can also occur in sewing patterns. The various pattern companies use different amounts of ease in the bust, waist, and hip areas. They may interpret the fit of various current styles quite differently. It's really all up to the individual designers and patternmakers who develop the styles.

As styles change, our concept of good fit changes also. Fashion may dictate that all clothing is so loose that everyone looks pregnant, or so tight that only the thinnest among us look good at all. Weight gain or loss, a pregnancy, an injury, or simply advancing age can all make your figure different and therefore more difficult to fit.

All these factors contribute to the confusion about good fit. The bewildering array of "sizes within a size" leaves you, the consumer and home sewer, in the midst of a fitting jungle. This book is designed to eliminate the confusion and help you achieve good fit. Whether you have an almost perfect figure or a real problem figure, you will have fitting problems at one time or another. And whether you have been sewing for years or have very limited sewing skills, this book will show you how to solve those fitting problems quickly and easily. It was developed as a fast, easy-to-use fitting primer for today's busy working woman, mother, or homemaker. It can show you how you can have attractive, well-fitting garments with a minimal expenditure of time and energy. Keep it handy!

Making Your Clothes FIT

Part I

General Instructions and Information

How to Use This Book

First carefully read the section below entitled "General Instructions and Information." Once you are familiar with this section, it will not be necessary to keep referring to it.

Try on your garment. Look at yourself in a full-length mirror, identify the problem area or areas, and then find the section of the book you need: Pants, Skirts, Blouses, Sleeves, or Dresses. Using the small drawings on the master guide at the beginning of each section, select the drawing that most closely approximates your "wrinkle" or "sag." Turn to the indicated page and follow the "sewing solution" if your garment is ready-made, or the "pattern solution" if you are working with a commercial pattern. While not all "wrinkles" can be solved with a sewing solution, most can be remedied in some way.

Simply follow the step-by-step instructions, and you will eliminate your wrinkle or sag in record time, without biting your nails or saying nasty words to your sewing machine.

General Instructions and Information

You will need some basic equipment to make fitting corrections. I find the following useful to have on hand:

"C-THRU Beveled Ruler" #B-85, 18"—a gridded ruler essential for making corrections on patterns.

"FASHION-METICS Fashion Ruler #670—a curve useful for correcting armholes, necklines, and hiplines.

"FAIRGATE" metal yardstick #110-T (or any good metal yardstick)—you need a perfectly straight edge that won't warp for pattern changes on large areas like pants legs and skirts.

"FAIRGATE" metal L-square in size you prefer, or a metal or plastic triangle 45 x 90—necessary for marking right angles at neckline and sleeve, etc.

#1 black lead pencil and a red erasable pencil—for marking patterns and corrections. As you gain confidence, you may want to switch to fine tip felt markers.

Plastic-coated tape measure—more accurate and durable than a cloth tape measure.

Paper scissors and cloth scissors.

Straight pins.

Tailors' chalk—for marking corrections on ready-made garments.

Transparent tape.

Roll of white tissue paper—for extending or changing patterns.

Round string or cord—when tied snugly around the waist it will roll automatically to your natural waistline, a great help in fitting procedures.

You may also find it useful to have weights to hold your pattern pieces securely on your table or desk as you work. Sand-filled beanbags work well and are inexpensive.

Explanation of Terms

There are several technical terms used throughout the book. Familiarize yourself with them before you start any correction.

Apex: The apex is the central point of the bust. All front bodice darts radiate from this point. In the back bodice, the darts radiate from the point of the shoulder blade.

Slash and pivot: This is the easiest method to move fullness from one location on a garment to another, and to establish new darts and close old ones. It simply means slashing with your scissors a specified place on a pattern, and swinging the pattern in a specified direction to move the fullness wherever you want. This method is also used to add fullness to a garment, by slashing and spreading, and to take out fullness, by slashing and overlapping. Always leave a small part of the pattern connected, unless specified otherwise.

Truing: Many pattern corrections leave the outside edge of the pattern distorted. Truing is simply straightening out the pattern edges again after the correction(s) have been made.

Wrinkle: Or tension pull. For the purpose of this book a wrinkle is defined as an area of a garment that pulls so tightly that horizontal or vertical ripples are produced.

Sag: A sag is an area of a garment that fits so loosely that the excess cloth gathers in horizontal or vertical folds.

Areas of Control

The "area of control" of a pattern is something that is very important and yet no pattern books ever mention it. Every part of a pattern is related to every other part of that same pattern. Yet each pattern line or edge exerts influence or control over a very specific area of fit. Study the pattern drawings below and try to memorize the information about the various areas of control. Once this knowledge becomes second nature to you, you will find yourself making fitting corrections almost instinctively.

Front and Back Bodice

Study the illustrations for a typical bodice below. Try to memorize the accompanying explanations. Once you thoroughly understand the various areas of control and have learned to read your wrinkles and sags correctly, you should be able to make almost any fitting correction.

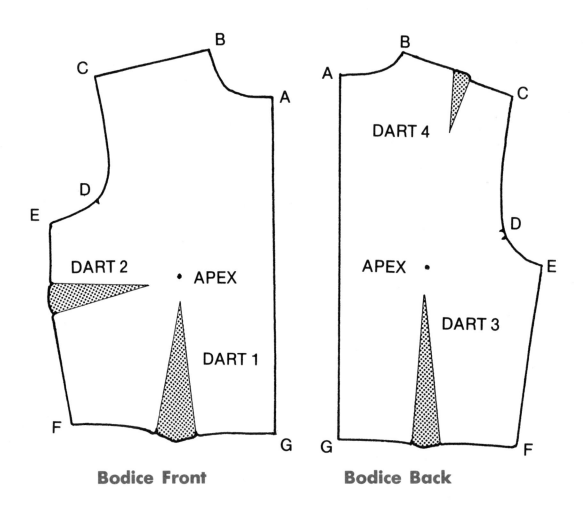

Bodice Front   **Bodice Back**

Line A-B: Controls neck size. A small dart in this area eliminates fullness and shapes in neckline. Lowering this line enlarges neckline.

Line B-C: Controls locations of shoulder seam. By raising or lowering point C you achieve a larger or smaller armhole. It is important that point C fall directly over the acromion, the knobby bone at the end of the shoulder, or you will have difficulty getting a proper sleeve fit. A small dart in the back bodice at B-C (see dart #4) not only shapes the shoulder but eliminates fullness from line C-D. On the front bodice at line C-D fullness can be eliminated with a small dart on a completed garment or slashed and pivoted into the side bust dart on a pattern.

Line C-E: Controls the size and shape of the armhole. Remember that moving point C changes the armhole by giving more or less shoulder room. **Please note:** Moving point E out enlarges the armhole too but also increases the chest measurement. Conversely, moving point E in decreases both the size of the armhole and the chest measurement. Any change in the size of the armhole must be accompanied by corresponding changes in sleeve size.

Line E-F: This line must be the correct length to insure a proper sleeve fit and waistline fit on garments with a waistline. Moving point G in or out can increase or decrease the waistline size, but dart #1 on the front bodice, and dart #3 on the back bodice, and line G-A also control waistline size. Any waistline corrections are generally divided equally between the bodice darts and side seams, and the center front or center back seam if the garment has them.

Line G-A: Moving line G-A not only increases waist, chest, and neckline size, but increases the distance between the darts and the armholes. Moving line G-A in decreases all these measurements.

Front and Back Pants

Study the illustrations for a typical pants front and back below, and try to memorize the accompanying explanations.

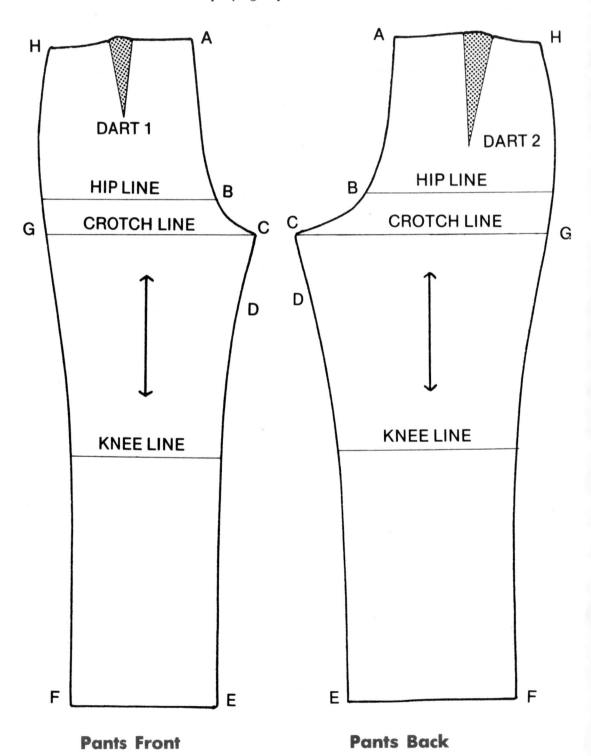

Pants Front   **Pants Back**

Line A-B: This line controls the crotch depth. This line can be lengthened or shortened by slashing and spreading or slashing and overlapping along the hipline.

Line B-C: The proper curve along this line is essential for a comfortable crotch fit. By moving point C in or out and blending into line C-E at point D the crotch can be shortened or lengthened while subtracting or adding from the area of thigh fit (line C-D) at the same time.

Line C-E: The Inseam. The position of this line along with line F-G determines how the pants leg will hang.

Line E-F: Controls the width of the pants leg.

Line F-G: The outseam. Controls how the pants leg will hang along with line C-E.

Line G-H: Controls the hip measurement. More or less curve will be required here depending on your figure. Darts #1 and #2 also control hip curve and affect waistline size.

Line H-A: Controls waistline size along with darts #1 and #2. Moving points H and A out or in will increase or decrease the size of the waistline. As on the bodice, any waistline corrections are generally divided between these points and the darts to help maintain the balance of the original pattern. Making a large correction on just one area of the pattern tends to distort the grainline and throw off dart positions and design details.

Please note: If you attempt to make the hip area smaller by taking up the seam along line A-B, you will also be making the crotch deeper if you continue the correction to point C. Unless you want a deeper crotch, it is best to make hip corrections along line G-H.

Fitted Sleeve

Study the illustrations for a typical fitted sleeve, and try to memorize the accompanying explanations.

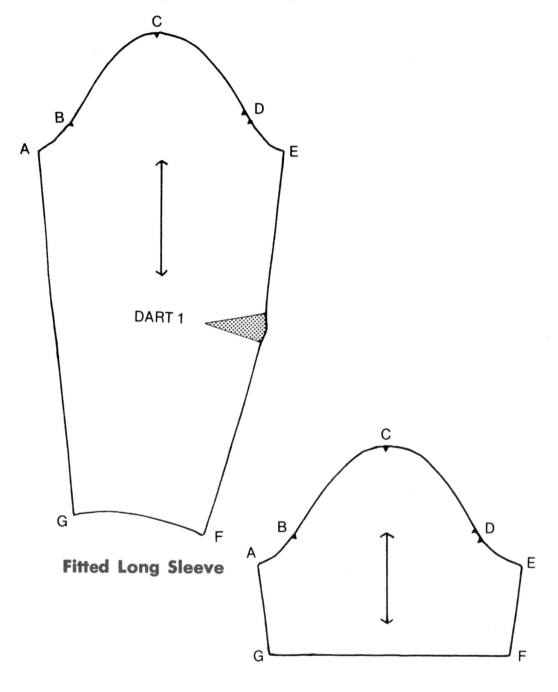

Fitted Long Sleeve

Fitted Short Sleeve

Lines A-B
and D-E: Control the length of the sleeve cap. Any
                change in the front or back bodice between
                points D and E should be matched by a corre-
                sponding change in sleeve lines A-B and D-E so
                that the sleeve will continue to fit the armhole.

Line B-C-D: Controls the height of the sleeve cap. Raising or
                lowering point C not only adds or subtracts
                height from the sleeve, but also makes the
                sleeve cap longer or shorter and adds width to
                the sleeve through the cap. Sleeve ease is
                always included in this area.

Lines E-F
and G-A: Control the length of the sleeves.

Line F-G: Controls the width of the sleeve.

Dart #1:   Adds ease and shape to the elbow area of a
                fitted sleeve.

Fitting Garments and Patterns

What is good fit? It is a garment that feels comfortable and looks good, that neither binds nor pulls, and has sufficient ease for movement without bagginess. It is seams that hang straight and don't hike up. It is darts that lay smoothly and don't pucker, with dart points that come just short of the apex of the bust and the shoulder blades.

How do you achieve good fit? You put your garment on inside out over the underclothing you will wear with it. Using this book and a mirror as guides, decide where you need to make changes. Since it is difficult to fit yourself properly in the back areas, have a friend who sews help you with those corrections. You can return the favor when she needs help. Use straight pins to pin up the corrections. If you are enlarging a garment, generally you will first need to rip the side seams and darts before you put it on to make corrections. When you are satisfied with the overall fit, mark the corrections with tailors' chalk. Take the garment off and restitch as necessary. Remember, not all corrections are completely successful on finished garments as you may not have enough material to effectively change the fit.

Since I am always in a hurry and always trying to save time when I sew, I use the following method to fit paper patterns before I cut them out in fabric. I simply compare my body measurements to those of the pattern, allowing approximately 2″ ease in the bust, 1″ in the waist, and 1½″ in the hips. These are pretty basic amounts for ease, but the amount you allow will depend on how you like your garments to fit. The tighter the fit, the less ease there is in a garment.

Decide which measurements you need for the style you are making. For example, for an empire-style dress you really only need the bust and underbust measurements, not the waist and hips. It's a good idea to *always* check sleeve length and cuff length before you cut. I once made a beautiful eyelet peasant blouse. When I put it on, my arms wouldn't fit through the cuffs on the puff sleeves. A thirty-second spot check of my upper arm measurement versus the pattern cuff measurement would have saved me a lot of ripping, swearing, and lost time. I haven't made that particular mistake again. You may find it handy to keep your measurements written on a card taped somewhere close to your sewing machine. Remember to check them from time to time for accuracy.

Crotch depth, pant, dress, and skirt length can all be checked easily before cutting, when corrections are easier to make. All commercial patterns feature lines for lengthening or shortening these measurements and instructions on how to do so.

As long as my measurements are smaller than the pattern measurements I am working with (including ease), I will cut out the garment, sew up all the major seams, and then put it on for a quick fitting session as I sew. I check my darts, the hang of the garment, and the feel of the garment. Any additional corrections that are needed I make as I sew. I am always careful to transfer these corrections back to the pattern as I am working so that the pattern will be right for future uses. If I make a larger dart or a smaller seam, these changes are noted on the pattern.

If the pattern you have purchased is too small when compared with your measurements, you must tape some white tissue paper to the pattern and add to it as necessary to achieve a good fit. After you have done this a few times, you will do as I do and buy a larger size pattern. It is easier to cut down a large pattern than to add to a small pattern. If you have two different size measurements, such as a size 10 waist with size 12 hips or bust, by all means buy the larger pattern and fit down to your smaller measurement. If you buy a size 12 for your bust, you can easily trim the waist down to a 10. But try buying a size 10 and adding to the bust to get a size 12 after you have cut out the garment. It sounds impossible and it is, but it is surprising how · many women try to do just that. If in doubt, buy the larger size!

A FEW POINTERS BEFORE YOU GET STARTED

* Do not fit your garment so tightly that you can't move! Take out the wrinkles and the sags, but leave the ease in!

* To facilitate the fitting of pants, skirts, and dresses with a waistline, tie a round cord around your waist. It will roll to your natural waistline, an important fitting reference point.

* Have all your equipment arranged in one place before you start. It will save you time in the long run.

* If you buy a garment with the idea of altering it, make sure the seam allowances are sufficiently wide to let out if necessary. Many garments today are made on an "overedge" machine, which sews a ¼"-wide finished seam and has a knife that trims off all the excess fabric outside the seam. This doesn't leave you much to work with in the way of seam. It is better to buy a bigger size in this case.

* Make corrections one at a time. A correction in one area will often solve an apparent problem in another area. Study your areas of control and how they relate to one another. Reading both the sewing and pattern solution will help you solve the problem more easily.

* If extra fullness lies close to a dart it can often be taken up in the dart on a finished garment. On a pattern the fullness can be pivoted into the dart.

* Press tissue patterns with a warm iron to remove wrinkles before you make any changes.

* All pattern lines must be trued after corrections have been made.

* To remove needle and hem marks, I wash the garment and drip dry it. While it is still damp, I steam iron the garment using a press cloth. Needle and hem marks will **not** come out of velvet, imitation suedes, real leathers, corduroys, and some finely woven synthetics. This is another good reason for buying a larger size. Seams that are taken up don't show. Seams that are let out often do.

ONE FINAL NOTE

I have tried to include all the most common fitting problems in this book, but I may have missed one or two. If you have a problem that does not appear in this book, go ahead and tackle it anyway. If you have a husband or children with fitting problems, you can solve them too with this book. Men and children are shaped differently than women, but the fitting principles remain the same. Once you master the concept of areas of control, you should feel confident and knowledgeable enough to make any fitting correction on any garment.

Try on the garment. Analyze the problem. Does the garment wrinkle or sag? Is it too tight or too loose? Try to determine the area of control for the problem. If the garment is too tight, see what effect ripping a seam or dart in the area of control will have. If the garment is too large, try enlarging the dart or adding a new dart or tuck in the area of control. By experimenting and using common sense and logic you can solve most of your fitting problems. Don't let wrinkles and sags intimidate you!

Part II

Sewing
and
Pattern
Corrections

Pants

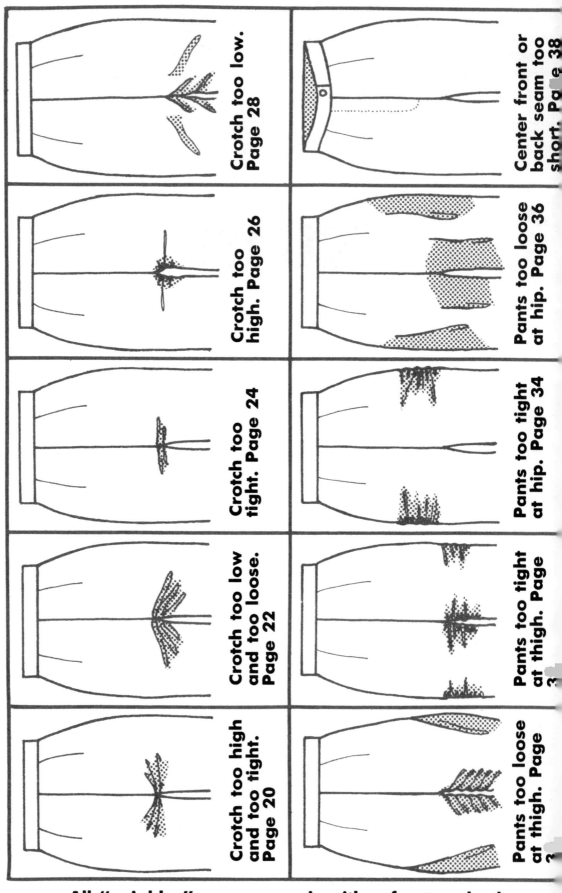

Crotch too low. Page 28

Center front or back seam too short. Page 38

Crotch too high. Page 26

Pants too loose at hip. Page 36

Crotch too tight. Page 24

Pants too tight at hip. Page 34

Crotch too low and too loose. Page 22

Pants too tight at thigh. Page 3

Crotch too high and too tight. Page 20

Pants too loose at thigh. Page 3

All "wrinkles" can appear in either front or back of pants, unless specified otherwise.

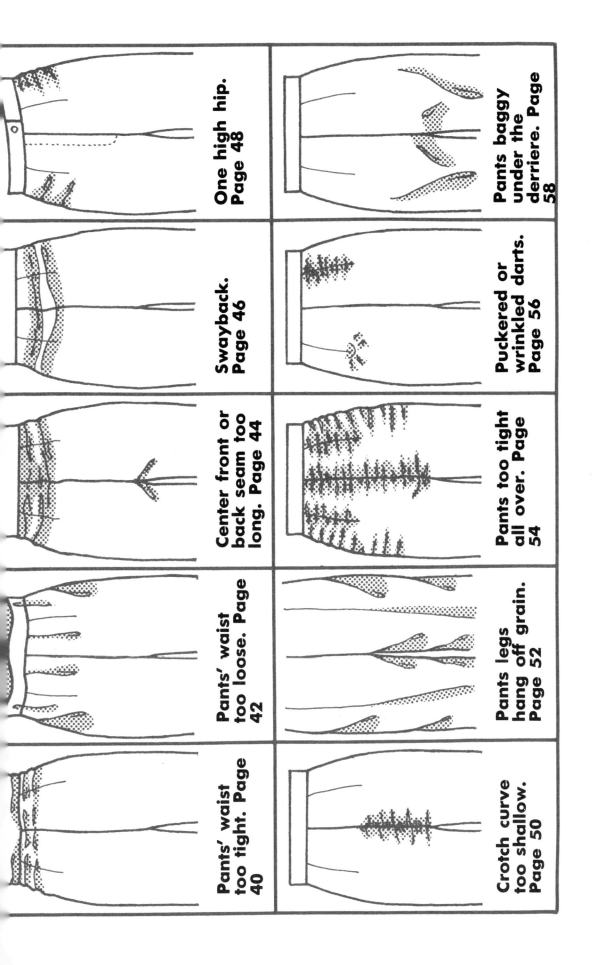

One high hip.
Page 48

Pants baggy under the derriere. Page 58

Swayback.
Page 46

Puckered or wrinkled darts.
Page 56

Center front or back seam too long. Page 44

Pants too tight all over. Page 54

Pants' waist too loose. Page 42

Pants legs hang off grain. Page 52

Pants' waist too tight. Page 40

Crotch curve too shallow. Page 50

SEWING SOLUTION   The crotch is too tight from point A to point B, and too high from point B to point C. Let out the seam from point A to point B as much as is possible. Lower the crotch from point B to point C to achieve a comfortable fit. Stitch a new seam as indicated by the dotted line below, blending into the front crotch if you're stitching from the back or vice versa. Trim off the shaded area.

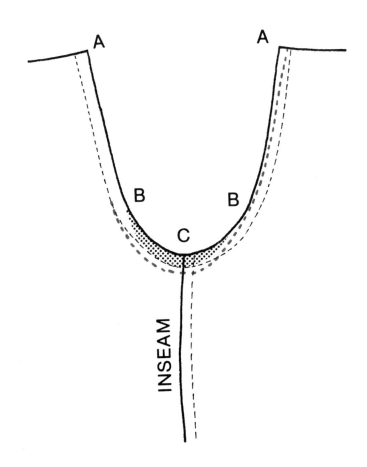

The old stitching line is shown in black, the new stitching line is shown in red. The material to be trimmed off is shown by shading.

PATTERN SOLUTION   Extend the pattern from point A to point B as much as you need to achieve a comfortable fit. Scoop out the crotch, blending the line in an even curve. You must scoop out the crotch on the opposite side of the pants an equal amount so that your inseams will still match. The dotted line on the drawing represents your new cutting line. Make the full correction on both front and back if you need it.

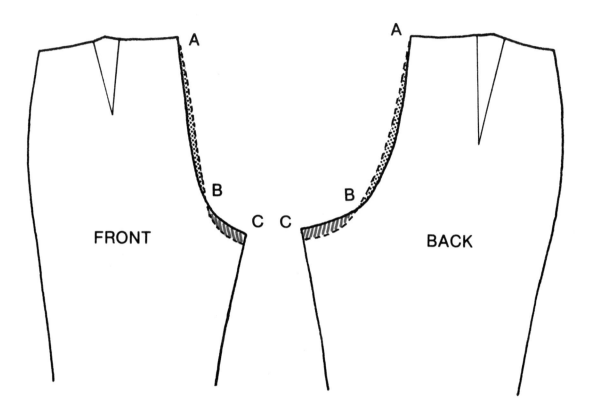

A
A
B
B
C C
FRONT
BACK

The area to be cut off is shown by red lines and the area to be added is shown by gray shading.

SEWING SOLUTION   *Please note:* This is a difficult correction. It is better to buy pants with a high crotch you can lower than pants with a low crotch you may *not* be able to raise.

The crotch is too loose from point A to point B and too low from point B to point C. Take up the seam from point A to point B as needed, but do not go beyond point B as you will be lowering the crotch even further. In order to raise the crotch, you must rip off the waistband and put the pants on inside out. (You can only do this if there is enough fabric in the pants hem to let down an amount equal to what you take up when you raise the pants at the waist.) Tie a round cord over the pants around your waist to establish your natural waistline. Lift the pants until the sags at the crotch disappear and the fit feels comfortable. Repin the darts and side seams if necessary for a good waist fit, and mark the corrections with tailors' chalk. Trim off excess fabric along waistline, being sure to leave a sufficient seam allowance. Resew darts and side seams. Reset waistband. Rehem legs.

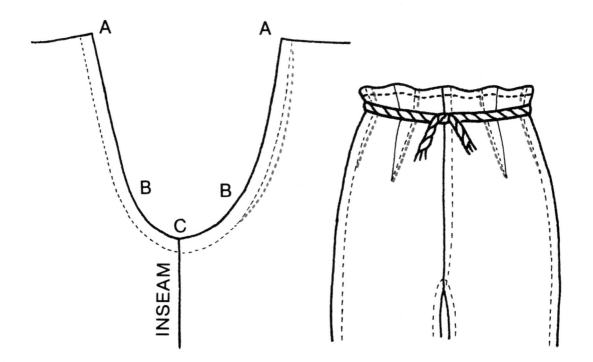

The old stitching line is shown in black, the new stitching line is shown in red. The material to be trimmed off is shown by shading.

PATTERN SOLUTION   Pare down the seam from point A to point B as
needed. Raise the crotch to achieve a comfortable fit between point B and
point C. Raise the crotch on the opposite side of the pants an equal amount
so that your inseams will still match. The dotted line on the drawing represents your new cutting line. Make the full correction on both front and back if
needed.

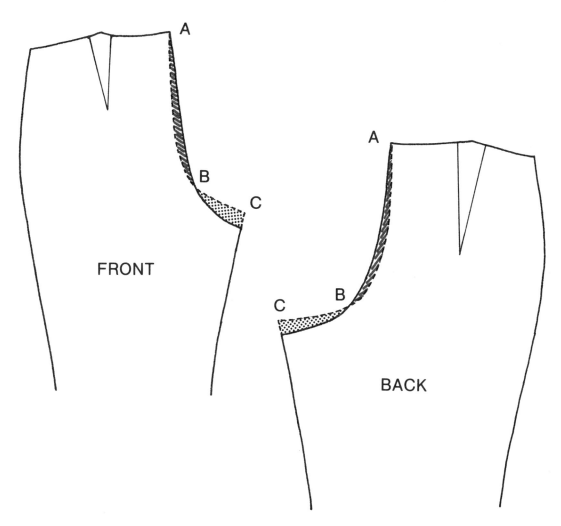

**The area to be cut off is shown
by red lines and the area to be
added is shown by gray shading.**

SEWING SOLUTION   The crotch is too tight between point A and point B which causes horizontal pulls directly beneath the derriere. Let out the seam between point A and point B as much as possible, blending your stitching line in. If this doesn't solve your problem entirely, try letting out a little on the inseams between points C and D.

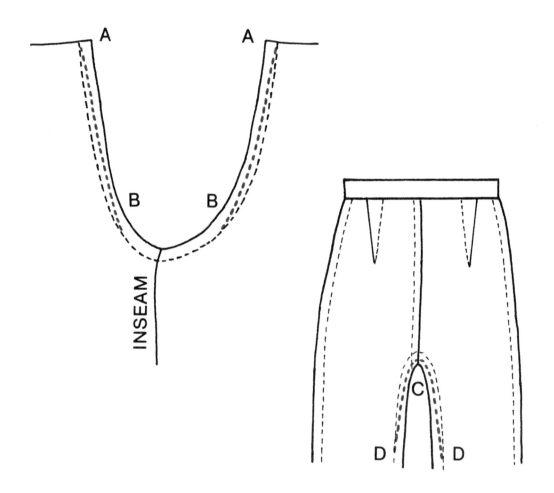

The old stitching line is shown in black and the new stitching line is shown in red.

PATTERN SOLUTION   Extend the pattern between points A and B, blending the line into a smooth curve. Make the correction on both front and back if needed. The dotted line is the new cutting line.

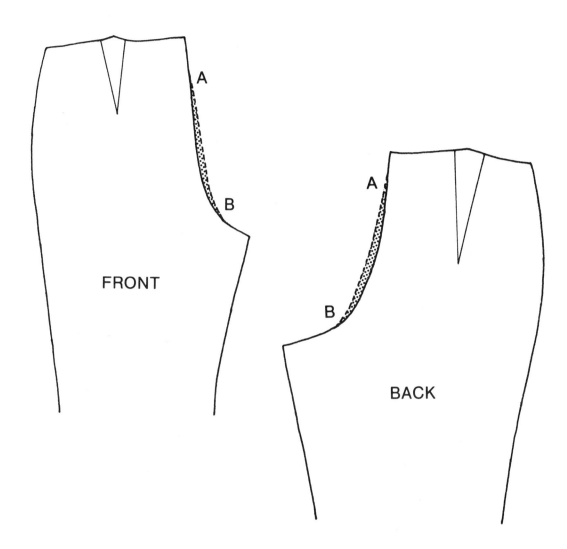

The area to be added is shown by gray shading.

SEWING SOLUTION   The crotch is too high and cuts uncomfortably into the body. Lower the stitching line between points B and C, blending into a smooth curve. Trim off the excess fabric as indicated by the shaded area. As you lower the crotch curve you are tightening the thigh area somewhat. If it feels tight or pulls after the crotch correction, let out the inseam between points C and D to compensate.

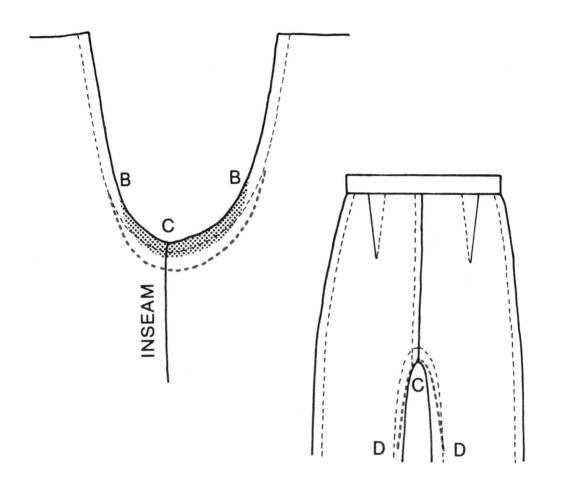

The old stitching line is shown in black, the new stitching line is shown in red. The material to be trimmed off is shown by shading.

PATTERN SOLUTION   Lower the crotch curve as indicated by the dotted line. Trim off the shaded area. If you lower the crotch more than ¾″ you should add a little to the thigh between points C and D to compensate for the thigh width you lose when you scoop out the crotch. Be sure to lower the front and back crotches an equal amount so that your inseams still match.

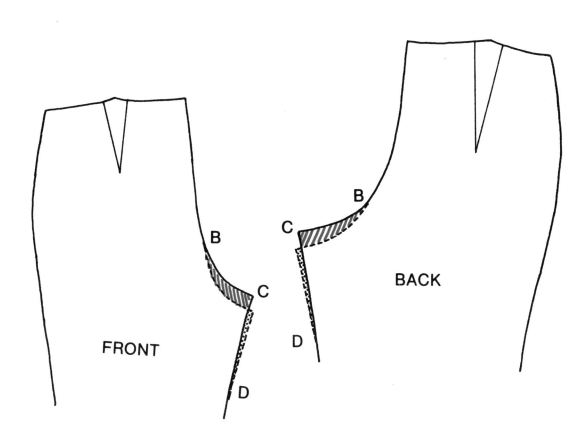

The area to be cut off is shown by red lines and the area to be added is shown by shading.

SEWING SOLUTION   *Please note*: This is a difficult sewing correction. It is better to buy pants with a high crotch that you can lower than pants with a low crotch that you may *not* be able to raise.

The crotch sags and feels uncomfortable. It falls below the level of your natural crotch and the skin of your thighs may chafe above the seam. Rip off the waistband and put the pants on inside out. (You can do this only if there is enough material in the pants hem to let down an amount equal to what you take up when you raise the pants at the waist.) Tie a round cord over the pants around your waist to establish your natural waistline. Lift the pants until all sags at the crotch disappear and the fit feels comfortable. Repin the darts and side seams if necessary for a good waist fit, and mark the corrections with tailors' chalk. Trim off excess fabric along waistline, being sure to leave a sufficient seam allowance. Resew darts and side seams. Reset waistband. Rehem legs.

The old stitching line is shown in black, the new stitching line is shown in red. The material to be trimmed off is shown by shading.

PATTERN SOLUTION   Raise the crotch from point B to point C as needed, blending the line into a smooth curve. Raise the front and back crotch an equal amount to keep the inseam lengths the same. You may want to pare a small amount from the leg between points C and D to keep the thigh measurement the same. The dotted line on the drawing represents the new cutting line.

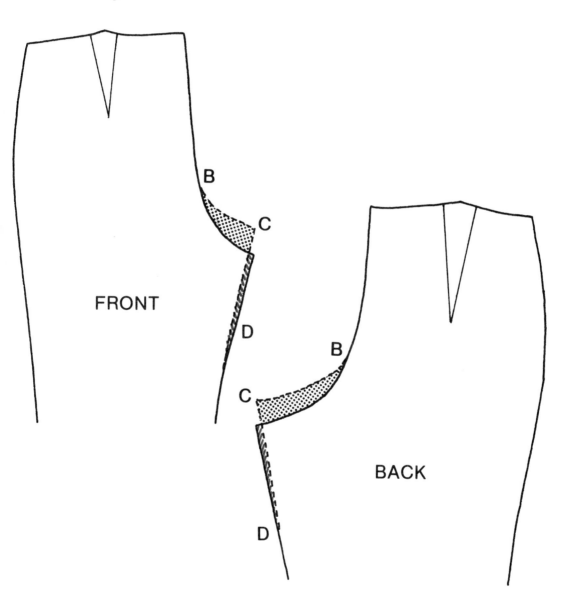

The area to be cut off is shown by red lines and the area to be added is shown by shading.

SEWING SOLUTION   Droopy folds on the inside of the thigh indicate a loose fit. If they are accompanied by a looseness or vertical folds on the outside of the thigh you will have to make a correction on both the inside and the outside of the leg. Take up the inside leg from point C to point D to achieve a better fit. But please keep in mind that as you take the thigh up, you are, in effect, also shortening the crotch. Take up the outseam as needed between points A and B. Trim off the excess material left after you make your corrections.

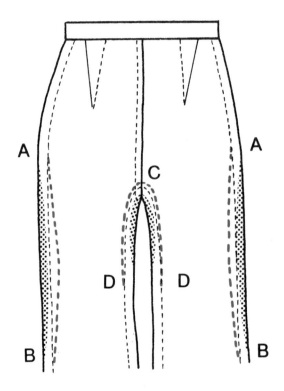

The old stitching line is shown in black, the new stitching line is shown in red. The material to be trimmed off is shown by shading.

PATTERN SOLUTION   Pare the leg down between points C and D on the inseam, and points A and B on the outseam. If you are making the correction on both sides of the leg try to keep the pattern balanced, that is, try to maintain the original contours of the pattern as you are cutting it down. The dotted line represents your new cutting line.

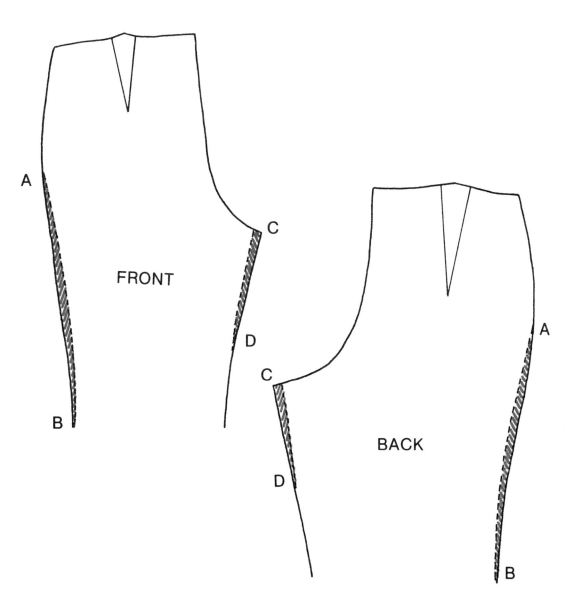

The area to be cut off is shown by red lines.

SEWING SOLUTION   Tension pulls at the thigh level on the inner and outer leg are an indication of a tight fit. Let out the inseam from point C to point D as needed, keeping in mind that this correction also lengthens the crotch somewhat. Let out the outseam from point A to point B, blending your new stitching line in with the old one.

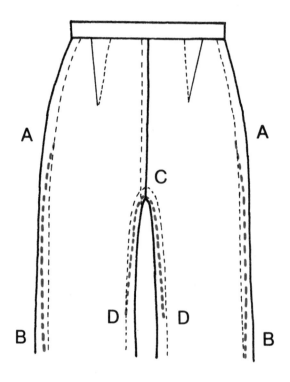

The old stitching line is shown in black, the new stitching line is shown in red.

PATTERN SOLUTION   Extend the leg outward on the inseam between point C and point D as much as you need for comfort. Extend the leg on the outseam between points A and B, maintaining the balance of the pattern, and the curve of the hip and thigh line. The dotted lines represent your new cutting lines.

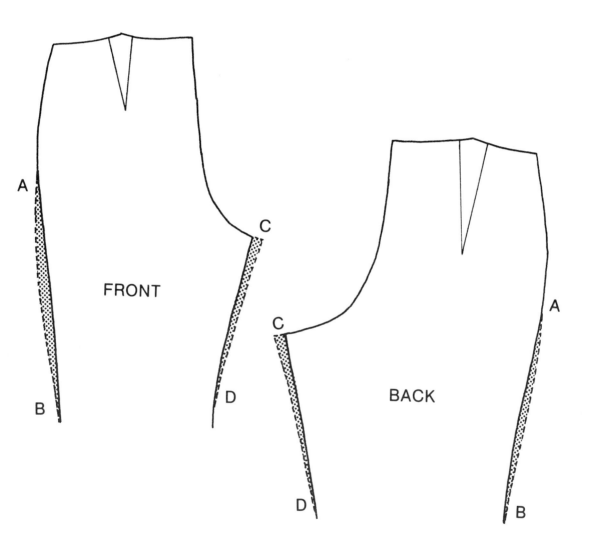

The area to be added is shown by shading.

SEWING SOLUTION   Tension pulls on the outseam at the hipline mean that the hips are too tight. Let out the seam from point A to point B as much as possible, blending the new stitching line into the old one.

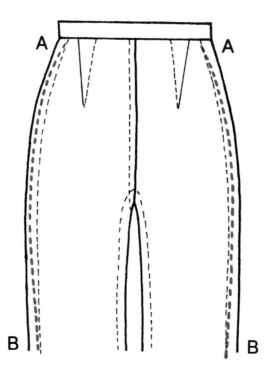

The old stitching line is shown in black, the new stitching line is shown in red.

PATTERN SOLUTION   Extend the outseam at the hipline between points A and C, keeping a smooth natural-looking curve at the hip. Add an equal amount to the front and back to keep the pattern balanced. For example, if you determine that you need a total correction of 1″, add ¼″ to the outseam of each of the two fronts and two backs. If you need to add more than 1″ total, simply extend the curve between point A and point B, coming back into the leg at point B. Keep all your lines smooth! The dotted line represents your new cutting line.

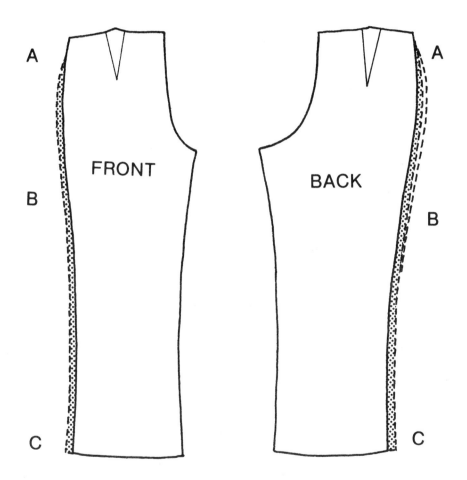

The area to be added is shown by shading. Additional area to be added is enclosed by a black broken line.

SEWING SOLUTION   If the pants are baggy all over and hang in vertical droops at the hipline, they are too loose in the hips. Starting at point A, take up the leg in a smooth line down to point C. You must let out the hem to do this. If the pants are still baggy, take up an additional amount between point A and point B, as needed. Trim off excess and rehem.

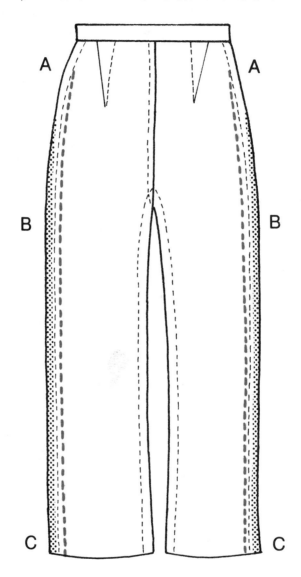

The old stitching line is shown in black, the new stitching line is shown in red. The material to be trimmed off is shown by shading.

PATTERN SOLUTION   Pare down the pattern between points A and C, taking off more between points A and B if needed. Be sure to take an equal amount off the front and back to keep the pattern balanced. The dotted line represents your new cutting line.

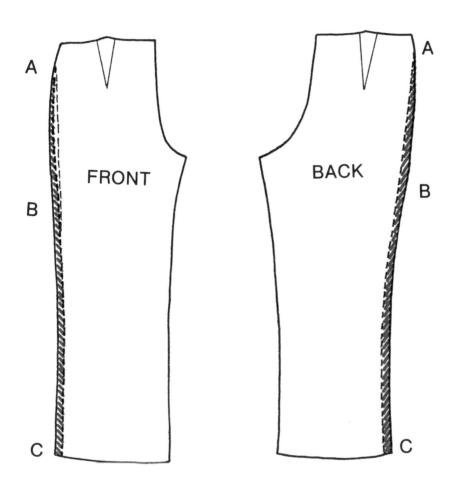

The area to be cut off is shown by red lines. Additional area to be cut off is enclosed by a black broken line.

SEWING SOLUTION   *Please note:* This is a difficult correction that can't always be made on a ready-to-wear garment.

The waistline dips down in the center front or center back or both because the crotch length is insufficient. Rip the waistband from side seam to side seam in the front or back (even if you must correct both front and back, leave the waistband attached at the side seams to serve as a guide). If there is enough fabric sewn into the waistband to allow you to make the correction, simply repin the waistband at the new level and resew. If there isn't enough material (and this is more common), you must rip the entire waistband. Try on the pants and estimate how much you need to bring up the center front or back. Take off the pants and lower the crotch by an equal amount, trimming

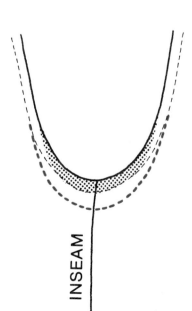

Use this correction if there is enough material sewn up in the waistband to correct the waistline dip.

The old stitching line is shown in black, the new stitching line is shown in red. The material to be trimmed off is shown by shading.

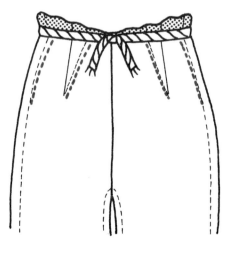

INSEAM

Use this correction if there is not enough fabric in the waistband to correct the waistline dip.

SEWING SOLUTION CONTINUED

the excess fabric away. Put the pants back on, inside out, and tie a round cord over the pants around your waist. The area being corrected should fall just under the cord while the side seams will stick up over the cord. Trim the excess fabric from the side areas. Repin the darts and side seams if necessary and mark with tailors' chalk. Resew the darts and side seams; reset the waistband. Lower the hems in the pants legs as necessary.

PATTERN SOLUTION   Slash the pattern along the hipline from A to B. Spread the amount you need to bring the center of the waistband up to the level of the waistband at the side seams. Tape a piece of tissue paper in the triangle-shaped wedge that results to hold the pattern in this new position. Don't make this correction in both front and back unless both front and back dip at the waistband.

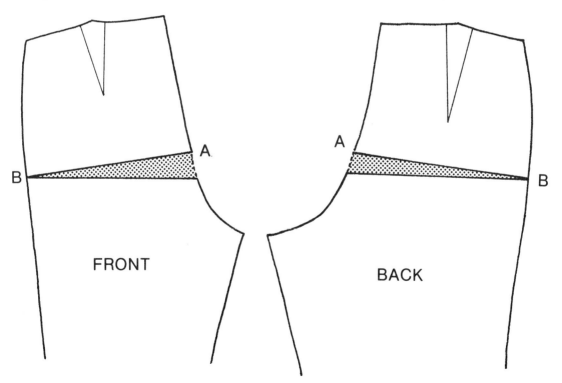

The area to be added is shown by shading.

SEWING SOLUTION   The waist is too tight. The waistband may buckle and roll over, and there are horizontal wrinkles beneath the waistband. Rip off the waistband. Let out the side seams and each of the darts as much as you need, dividing the correction equally between these areas. Repin the waistband. You may have to add a piece to the waistband if you don't have enough seam allowance to let out. A piece may be added on the under part of the button lap without showing at all. See drawing. Resew waistband.

The old stitching line is shown in black, the new stitching line is shown in red. The piece to be added is shown by shading.

PATTERN SOLUTION   Add to the waistline from point A to point B. Make your darts smaller. Be sure to divide your correction between the side seams and the darts to maintain the balance of the pattern. Whatever you add to the waistline must be added in an equal amount to the waistband. The dotted lines represent your new cutting lines.

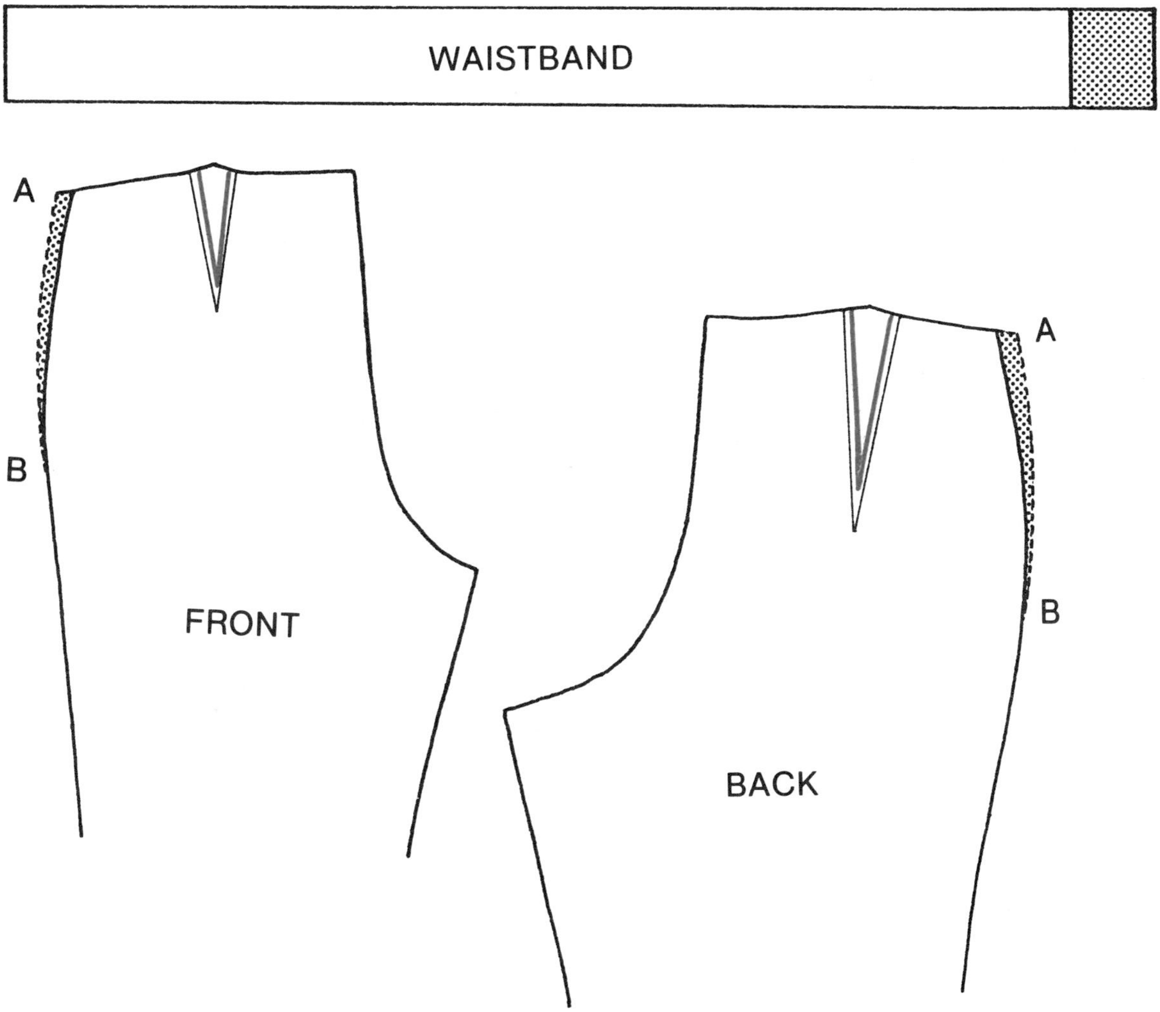

WAISTBAND

FRONT

BACK

The area to be added is shown by shading. New dart lines are shown in red.

SEWING SOLUTION   The waist is too loose. The waistband stands away from the body, and the pants fall in vertical folds directly beneath the waistband. Rip off the waistband. Take up the side seams and each of the darts as much as you need, dividing the correction equally between these areas. Trim off the excess fabric on the side seams. Repin the waistband. Trim off any excess. Resew the waistband.

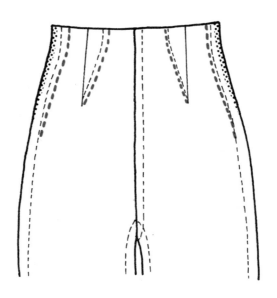

The old stitching line is shown in black, the new stitching line is shown in red. Material to be trimmed off is shown by shading.

PATTERN SOLUTION   Take in the waistline from point A to point B. Make your darts larger. Be sure to divide your correction between the side seams and the darts to maintain the balance of the pattern. Whatever you take out of the waistline measurement must be subtracted in an equal amount from the waistband. The dotted lines represent your new cutting lines.

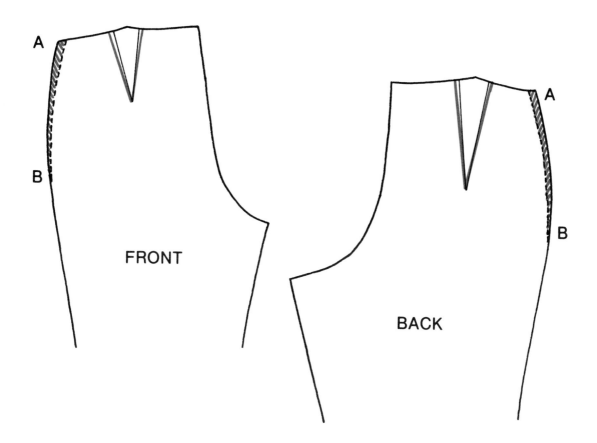

The area to be cut off is shown by red lines. New dart lines are shown in red.

SEWING SOLUTION   The waistband fits, but directly beneath the waistband there are horizontal folds of extra fabric. The crotch may droop a little. This means the center back or front seam is too long. Rip off the waistband from side seam to side seam in the affected area. Put the pants on inside out. Tie a round cord around your waist on top of the pants. Pull up the fabric in the affected area until the wrinkles disappear. Repin the darts if necessary to maintain good waistline fit and mark with tailors' chalk. Trim off excess fabric at center front or center back waistline. Take off pants. Resew darts, reset waistband. Make this correction in front and back only if needed in both locations.

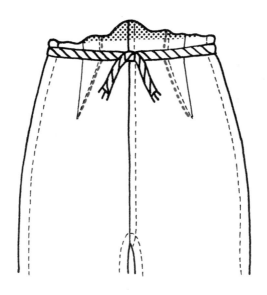

The old stitching line is shown in black, the new stitching line is shown in red. Material to be trimmed off is shown by shading.

PATTERN SOLUTION   Slash the pattern along the hipline from A to B. Overlap the amount you need to eliminate the excess fabric beneath the waistband. True the crotchline. The shaded area shows the overlap. Tape the pattern in this new position. Don't make this correction in both front and back unless needed.

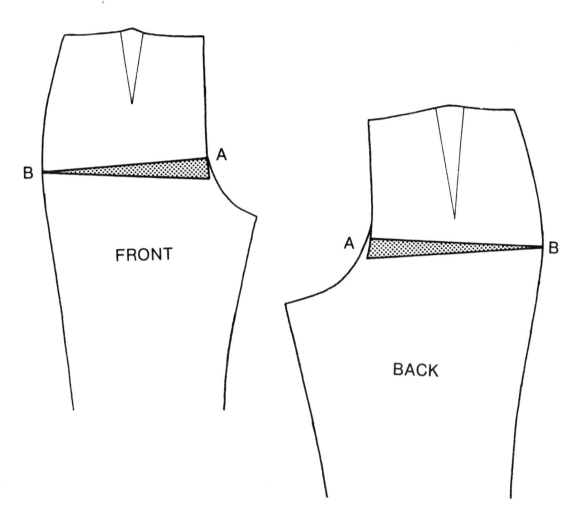

The area to be overlapped is shown by shading.

SEWING SOLUTION   There are one or two distinct horizontal pleats beneath the back waistband. Rip off the waistband from side seam to side seam in the back. Put the pants on inside out. Pull the fabric up in the affected area until the pleats disappear. Repin the waistband. (If you are very swaybacked, you may have to rip beyond the side seams toward the front and start lifting up the fabric there.) Take off the pants. Trim off the excess fabric around the waistline, leaving a sufficient seam allowance to reset the band. Resew the waistband.

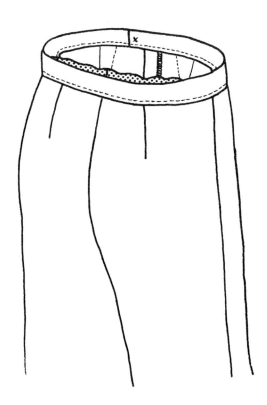

Material to be trimmed off is shown by shading.

PATTERN SOLUTION   Estimate how much you need to pull up in the center back to eliminate the horizontal pleats. Mark this amount on the center back of your pattern, approximately point A. Using your fashion curve, draw from point A up to point B at the side seams. You should get a curve resembling the one in the drawing below. The dotted line represents your new cutting line. Reposition your darts as shown if necessary to keep them straight.

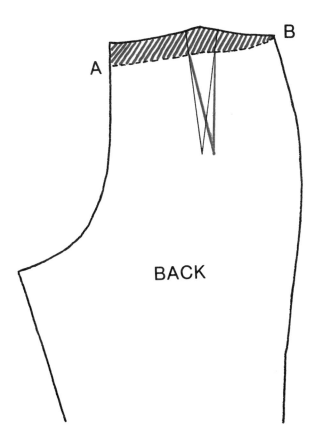

The area to be cut off is shown by red lines. New dart lines are shown in red.

SEWING SOLUTION   The pants pull over the higher hip and sag over the lower one. The waistband may seem to be askew. The crease on the low side generally hangs toward the inseam. Rip off the waistband. Rip the darts and 4–5″ of the side seam on the high side. Put the pants on inside out. Repin the darts and side seam on the high side letting out enough to eliminate the wrinkles. Take up the darts and side seam on the low side with pins, until the fit feels comfortable. Mark these corrections with tailors' chalk. Tie a round cord around your waist over the pants. Lift the side seam on the low side under the cord until the last sags disappear. Mark this new waistline. Repin the waistband and resew. Make corrections on both front and back.

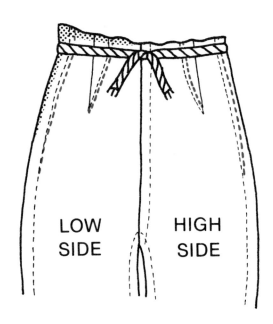

The old stitching line is shown in black, the new stitching line is shown in red. Material to be trimmed off is shown by shading.

PATTERN SOLUTION   Cut the entire pattern, front and back, in tissue paper again. One will serve as your high side pattern, and the other as your low side pattern. Determine how much you have to lift the pattern on the low side to eliminate the sags. Mark this on the pattern, approximately point A. You may also need to take up the darts and the side seams a little on the low side to maintain good waist fit. On the high side, let out the darts and side seam a little to eliminate wrinkling beneath the waistband. Use your fashion curve to draw a line from point A up to point B at the center back and the center front on the low side.

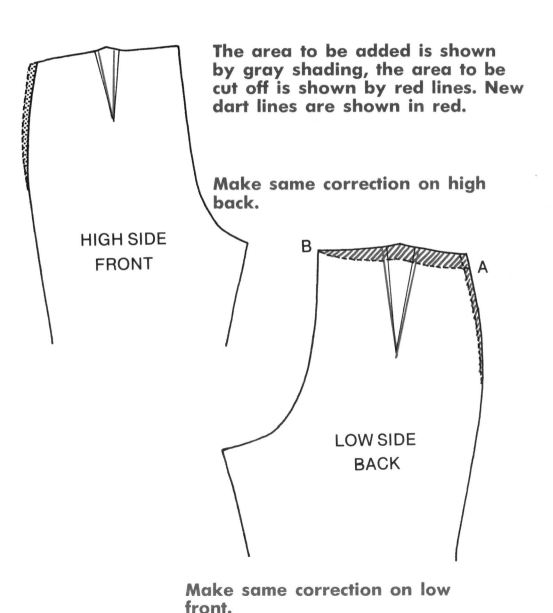

The area to be added is shown by gray shading, the area to be cut off is shown by red lines. New dart lines are shown in red.

Make same correction on high back.

HIGH SIDE
FRONT

B   A

LOW SIDE
BACK

Make same correction on low front.

SEWING SOLUTION   Horizontal pulls along the center front seam in the area of the pubis or along the curve of the derriere in the center back are an indication of a crotch curve that is too shallow. This defect usually causes an uncomfortable, somewhat binding fit. The solution is easy. Simply scoop out the crotch in the area of the curve, as indicated in the drawing. Blend your new stitching line smoothly into the old one, and trim off the excess fabric that results in the crotch curve.

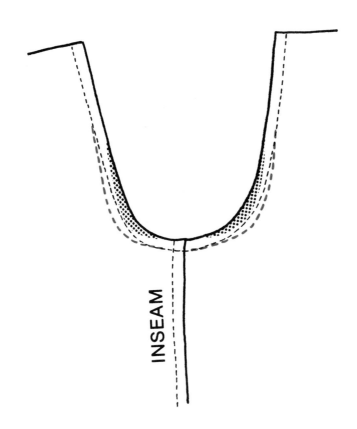

INSEAM

The old stitching line is shown in black, the new stitching line is shown in red. Material to be trimmed off is shown by shading.

PATTERN SOLUTION   Scoop out the crotch in the area of the curve, from point A to point B. Make the correction both in front and back only if you need it. Trim off the shaded area. The dotted line represents your new cutting line.

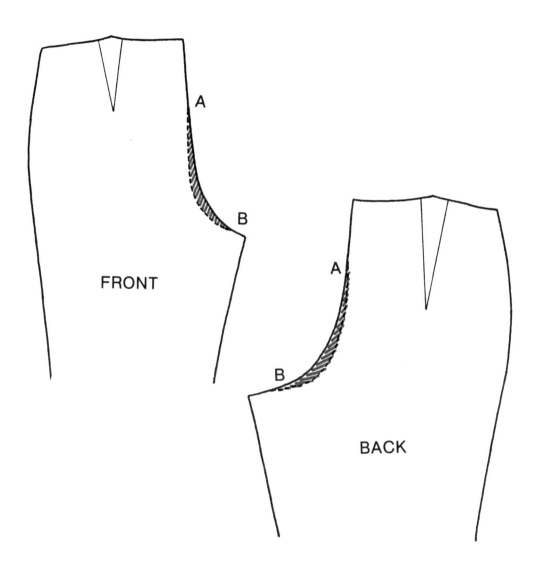

The area to be cut off is shown by red lines.

SEWING SOLUTION   *Please note:* This can be a real problem to correct if it is caused by the pants being badly cut at the factory. There may be almost no way to get them to hang on the grain again. If the problem is caused by a difference in your hips, it is relatively easy to correct.

When the pants' creases do not hang straight, and the pants droop and sag toward the inside of the leg, it is an indication that the pants are off grain. The correction given here will not solve the problem if the pants are cut badly to begin with. Rip off the waistband. Put the pants on inside out. Tie a round cord around your waist over the pants. Lift the pants on the side that droops until the crease hangs straight and the sags have disappeared. (Do both sides if needed.) Mark the new waistline with tailors' chalk. Trim off the excess fabric that results above the cord, leaving a sufficient seam allowance. Repin the waistband. Take off the pants and resew the waistband.

Material to be trimmed off is shown by shading.

PATTERN SOLUTION   Slash the pattern along the hipline, from point A to point B, and overlap the pieces as much as you need to make the leg hang straight. You may have to experiment to find the proper amount of overlap unless you have the pants already made up in muslin and can judge from that. If you are knock-kneed or have wide hips with legs set at the very outside of your hips, this can also make your pants hang improperly. Follow the second drawing. Slash the pattern completely apart on the kneeline and move the lower half in the direction of the inseam. Redraw your seam lines, maintaining the curve of the original pattern. This correction will also require some experimentation before your pants hang just right.

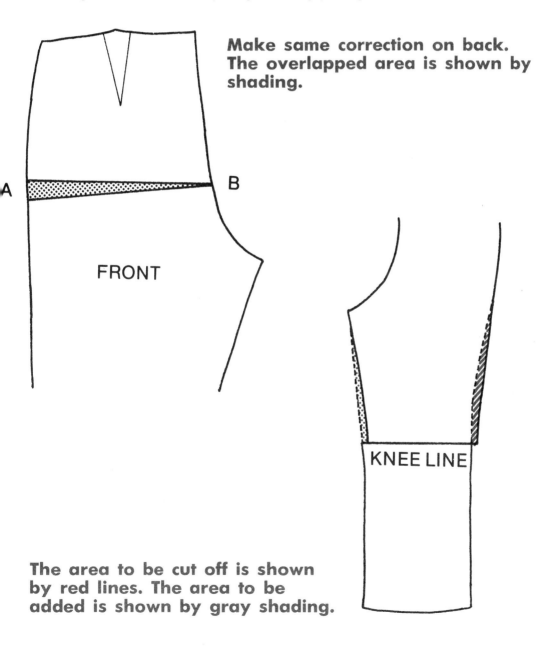

Make same correction on back. The overlapped area is shown by shading.

A

B

FRONT

KNEE LINE

The area to be cut off is shown by red lines. The area to be added is shown by gray shading.

SEWING SOLUTION   The pants have tight pulls all over the front if you have a tummy problem, or all over the back if you have a large derriere. If the pants pull both front and back, please consider buying a larger size! There is not much you can do for this correction except let out your side seams, center front or center back seam, and darts as much as possible without affecting your waistline measurement. Sewing your darts in a concave rather than a straight line may help. (See drawing.) All these corrections still may not give you enough fabric to completely eliminate your wrinkles, but they should help!

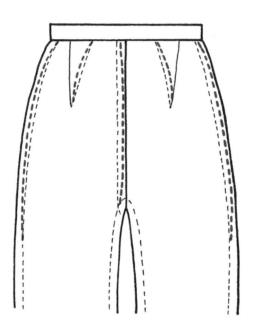

The old stitching line is shown in black, the new stitching line is shown in red.

PATTERN SOLUTION   The correction is the same whether done in front for the tummy or in back for the derriere. Slash the pattern from point A to point C, and from point D to point B. Slash from point E to point F. Slash from point G to point H. Arrange the pattern pieces as shown. The shaded area represents the amount of fabric you have gained without changing your waistline measurement. If your tummy is particularly rounded, or your buttocks very prominent, you should shorten your darts about ½″ and sew them in a concave shape as shown. Tape the pattern over tissue paper in the new position.

The area to be added is shown by gray shading. The area to be cut off is shown by red lines. New dart lines are shown in red.

SEWING SOLUTION   Darts that pucker at the end are too long. Darts that wrinkle are too tight. For a puckered dart, simply shorten the point of the dart at least ½″ and restitch, blending into the existing stitching line at the waist. For a dart that wrinkles, restitch the dart in a concave line as shown in the drawing. Rip out the old stitching line.

Puckered dart

Wrinkled dart

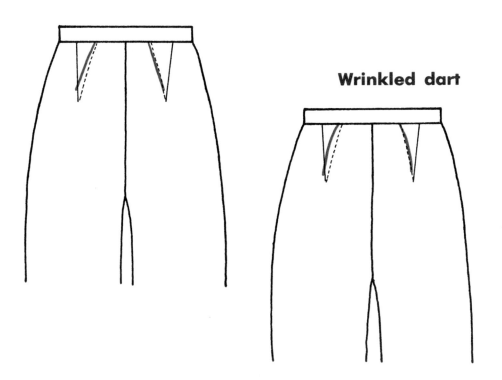

New dart lines are shown in red.

PATTERN SOLUTION   For a puckered dart, shorten the point of the dart at least ½″ and redraw, connecting points A and B. For a wrinkled dart, change the shape of the dart from straight to concave as indicated on the drawing.

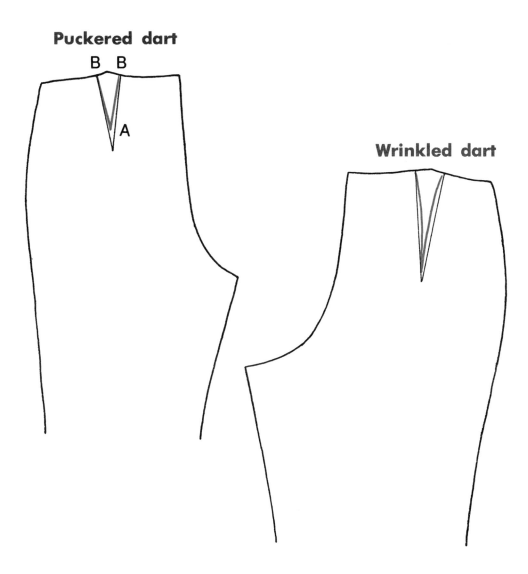

New dart lines are shown in red.

SEWING SOLUTION   Pants droop and sag directly under the buttocks in the back. This is caused by either an extremely small or flat derriere. Put the pants on inside out. Pin a diamond-shaped dart directly under the curve of the seat. This serves to mold the fabric under the seat and gives a curvier appearance. Mark the darts with tailors' chalk. If the pants are still baggy-looking, take up the side seams from point A to point B. Take off the pants and restitch the side seams, and sew up the darts.

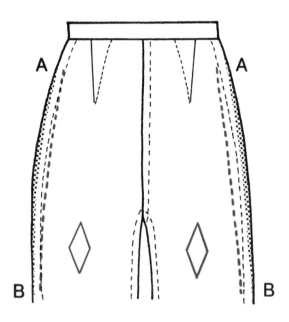

The old stitching line is shown in black, the new stitching lines and new dart lines are shown in red. Material to be trimmed off is shown by shading.

PATTERN SOLUTION   Using the crotchline as a guide, mark a diamond-shaped dart in the center of the pants' back. This dart should not be over 3″ long, and usually no more than 2″ wide. This will shape and curve the pants under your derriere, giving you a more rounded appearance. If you still feel that you need to take more off the pants, pare it from the side seams between points A and B on both the front and back patterns. The dotted line is your new cutting line.

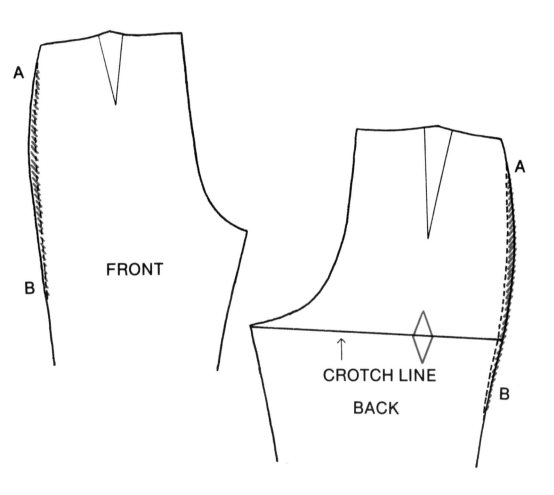

The area to be cut off is shown by red lines. New dart lines are shown in red.

Skirts

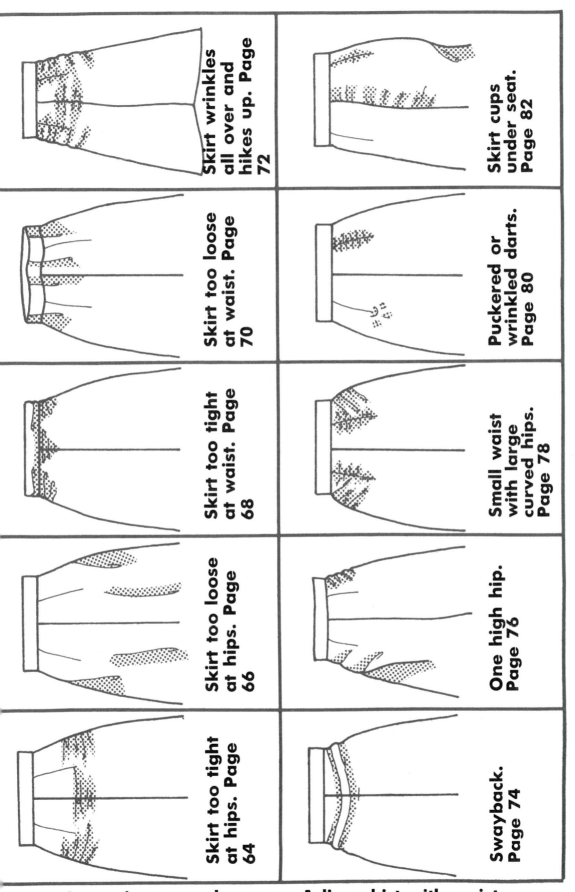

Skirt wrinkles all over and hikes up. Page 72

Skirt cups under seat. Page 82

Skirt too loose at waist. Page 70

Puckered or wrinkled darts. Page 80

Skirt too tight at waist. Page 68

Small waist with large curved hips. Page 78

Skirt too loose at hips. Page 66

One high hip. Page 76

Skirt too tight at hips. Page 64

Swayback. Page 74

Corrections are shown on A-line skirt with waist-band but may be used on all fitted skirts.

SEWING SOLUTION   Horizontal pulls at hip level are an indication of a skirt that is too tight through the hips. Let out the skirt from point A to point B on the side seams as much as possible. You may have to rip the hem at the side seams to do this. If you still need more room, let out the skirt from point C to point D on the center front or center back seam, whichever one does *not* have the closing. Divide your correction between these seams. Rehem if necessary.

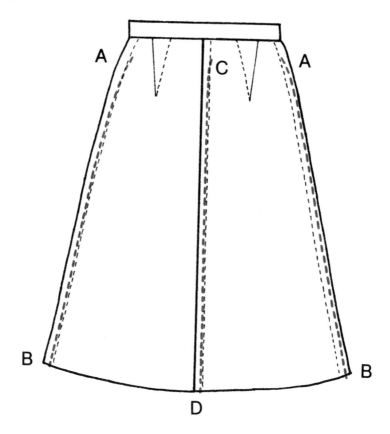

The old stitching line is shown in black, the new stitching line is shown in red.

PATTERN SOLUTION   Add to the side seams of both front and back an equal amount from point A to point B. Use your fashion curve to maintain a natural-looking hip curve as you do this. Add enough so that the skirt will hang smoothly over the curve of your hips without wrinkles. The dotted lines represent your new cutting lines.

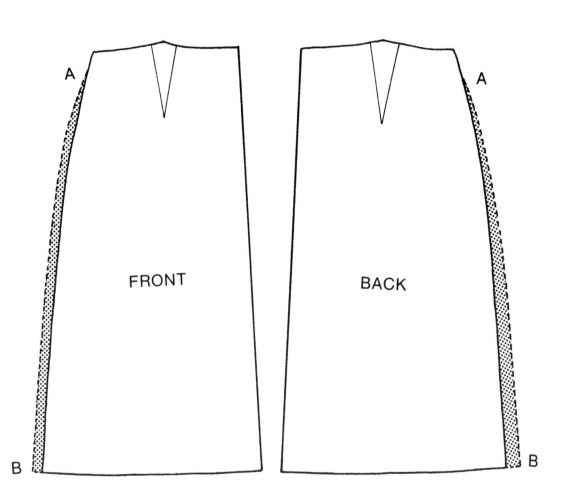

The area to be added is shown by shading.

SEWING SOLUTION   Vertical droops over the hips and through the length of the skirt are an indication of a skirt that is too loose through the hips. Starting at point A, take the side seams up enough to eliminate the sags, continuing in a smooth even line down to point B. You will have to rip a small part of the hem to do this. Divide the correction evenly between the side seams. Trim the excess fabric from the side seams after the corrections have been made, and rehem skirt.

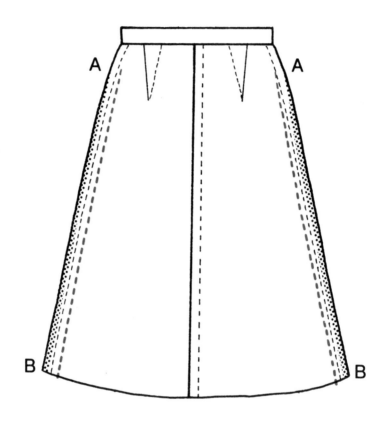

The old stitching line is shown in black, the new stitching line is shown in red. Material to be trimmed off is shown by shading.

PATTERN SOLUTION   Pare down the skirt, front and back, from point A to point B, using your fashion curve to maintain a natural-looking hip curve. Divide the correction evenly between front and back. Cut off enough to eliminate the sags. The dotted lines represent your new cutting lines.

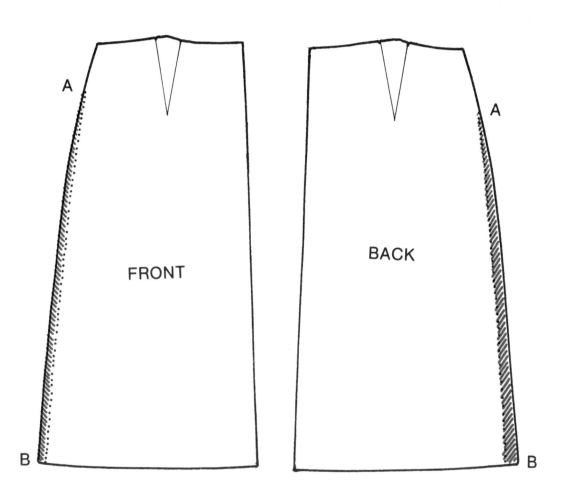

The area to be cut off is shown by red lines.

SEWING SOLUTION   A waistband that buckles and wrinkles horizontally directly beneath the waistband are indications of tight waist fit. Rip off the waistband. Let out the side seams and each of the four darts as much as necessary to obtain a smooth fit. Divide your correction evenly between all these areas to maintain the balance of the skirt. You may have to add a piece to the waistband after letting out the seams and darts, but if you add it to the inside part of the button lap it won't show. Reset the waistband.

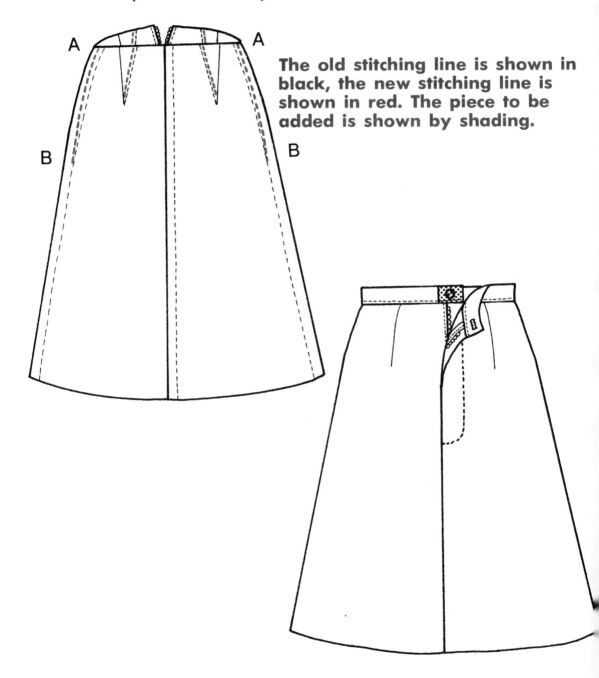

The old stitching line is shown in black, the new stitching line is shown in red. The piece to be added is shown by shading.

PATTERN SOLUTION   Add to the waistline, both front and back, between points A and B, using your fashion ruler to maintain a nice curve. Make the front and back darts smaller. Be sure to divide your correction between the side seams and the darts to maintain the balance of the pattern. Whatever you add to the waistline must be added in an equal amount to the waistband. The dotted lines represent your new cutting lines.

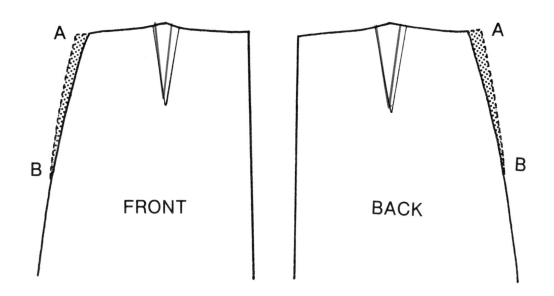

The area to be added is shown by shading. New dart lines are shown in red.

SEWING SOLUTION   When the waistband stands away from the body and the skirt falls in vertical folds directly beneath the waistband, the skirt waistline is too big. Rip off the waistband. Take up the side seams and each of the darts as much as you need to eliminate the sags and achieve a good waistline fit. Divide the correction evenly between the side seams and darts to maintain the balance of the skirt. Trim off the excess fabric on the side seams. Repin the waistband. Trim off any excess. Reset the waistband.

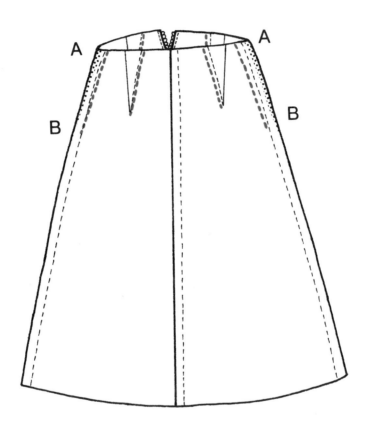

The old stitching line is shown in black, the new stitching line is shown in red.

PATTERN SOLUTION   Take in the waistline from point A to point B. Make your darts larger. Make the same correction both front and back to maintain pattern balance. Whatever you take out of the waistline measurement must be subtracted in equal amount from the waistband. The dotted lines represent your new cutting lines.

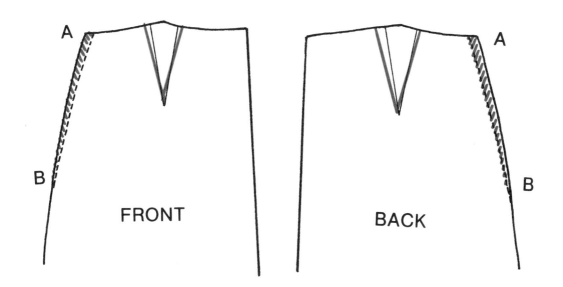

The area to be cut off is shown by red lines. New dart lines are shown in red.

SEWING SOLUTION   If you have a large tummy, the skirt will have horizontal pulls all across the front. The same pulls will appear in the back if you have a large derriere. If the skirt pulls both front and back, you should buy a larger size. You must let out the side seams, center front or back seams, and the darts as much as possible without affecting your waistline measurement. Sew your darts in a concave rather than a straight line. (See drawing.) *Please note*: All these corrections still may not give you enough fabric to completely eliminate the wrinkles.

The old stitching line is shown in black, the new stitching line and new dart lines are shown in red.

PATTERN SOLUTION   The correction is the same whether done in front for the tummy or in back for the derriere. Slash the pattern from point A to point C. Slash through the dart from point D to point B. Arrange the pattern pieces as shown and tape in new position over a piece of tissue paper. Notice that you are opening up your dart and making it larger. This will give the dart more shape. If your tummy is particularly rounded, or your buttocks very prominent, you should shorten your darts about ½″ and sew them in a concave shape as shown. The shaded area represents the amount of room you have gained without changing your waistline size. Use your fashion curve to reshape the hipline. The dotted line is the new cutting line.

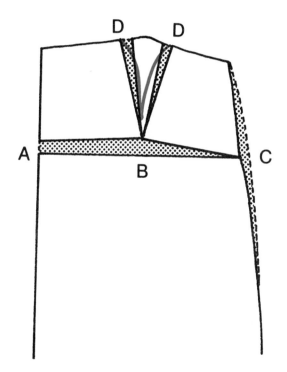

The area to be added is shown by shading. New dart lines are shown in red.

SEWING SOLUTION   One or two distinct horizontal pleats in back directly beneath the waistband are indicative of a swayback. Rip the waistband from side seam to side seam in the back. Put the skirt on inside out. Pull up the fabric in the affected area until the pleats disappear. Repin the waistband. (If you are very swaybacked, you may have to rip beyond the side seams toward the front and start lifting up the fabric there.) Take off the skirt and trim the excess fabric around the waistline, leaving a sufficient seam allowance to reset the band. Resew the waistband. *Note:* If the skirt has a back closing, you will have to lower the zipper to make this correction.

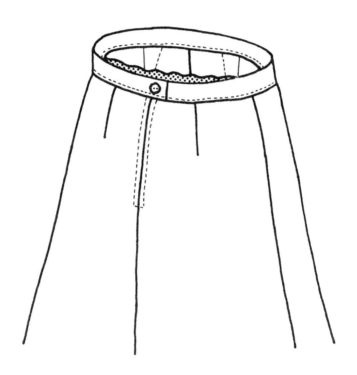

Material to be cut off is shown by shading.

PATTERN SOLUTION   Estimate how much you need to pull up in the center back to eliminate the horizontal pleats. Mark this amount on the center back of your pattern, approximately point A. Using your fashion curve, draw a line from point A up to point B at the side seam. You should get a curve resembling the one in the drawing below. The dotted line represents your new cutting line. Reposition your darts as shown if necessary to keep them straight.

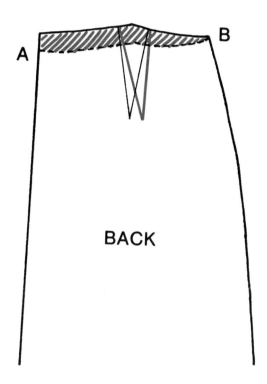

The area to be cut off is shown by red lines. New dart lines are shown in red.

SEWING SOLUTION   If the skirt pulls over one hip and sags over the other, it is an indication that you have one hip higher than the other. The center front and center back seams will probably hang off grain, skewing toward the high side. Rip the waistband off. Rip the darts and 4–5″ of the side seam on the high side. Put the skirt on inside out. Repin the darts and side seam on the high side, letting out enough to eliminate the wrinkles. Take up the darts and side seam on the low side until the fit feels comfortable. Mark these corrections with tailors' chalk. Tie a round cord around your waist over the skirt. Lift the side seam on the low side under the cord until the last sags disappear and the center seams hang straight. Mark this new waistline. Repin the waistband and resew. Make corrections on both front and back.

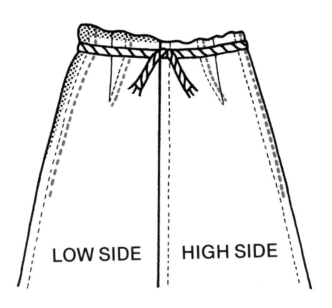

LOW SIDE   HIGH SIDE

The old stitching line is shown in black, the new stitching line is shown in red. Material to be trimmed off is shown by shading.

PATTERN SOLUTION   Cut the entire pattern, front and back, in tissue paper again. One set of tissues will serve as your high-side pattern, and the other set as your low-side pattern. Determine how much you have to lift the pattern on the low side to eliminate the sags and make the center seams hang straight. Mark this on both the front and back patterns, approximately point A. You may also need to take up the darts and the side seams a little on the low side to maintain good waist fit. On the high side, let out the darts and side seam a little to eliminate the pulls beneath the waistband. Use your fashion curve to draw a line from point A up to point B at the center back and the center front on the low side.

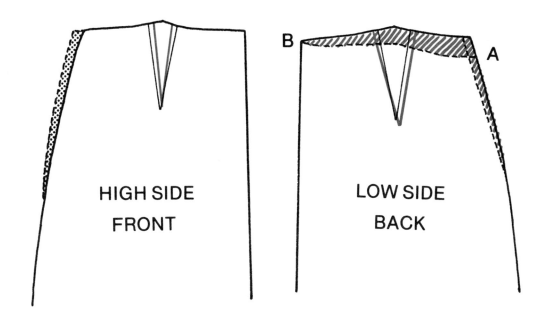

HIGH SIDE
FRONT

LOW SIDE
BACK

Make same correction on high back.   **Make same correction on low front.**

The area to be cut off is shown by red lines. The area to be added is shown by gray shading. New dart lines are shown in red.

SEWING SOLUTION   If your waist is small in comparison with your hips and your hips are particularly rounded, you will get diagonal pulls from the side seams and puckers across the darts on both the back and front of your skirt. Let out the side seams from point A to point B. Sew all four darts in a concave shape as shown in the drawing. All these corrections still may not give you enough room and eliminate the wrinkles if you have very large round hips and have bought the skirt to fit your waist.

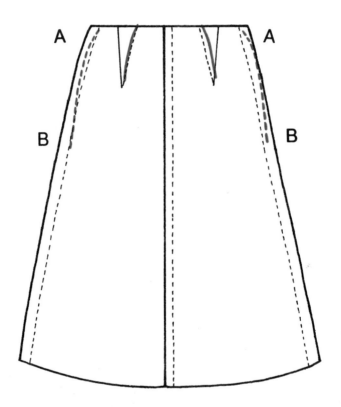

The old stitching line is shown in black, the new stitching line and new dart lines are shown in red.

PATTERN CORRECTION   Redraw your darts in a concave shape. Using your fashion curve, add from point A to point B on the front and back side seams, trying to approximate the natural curve of your own hips. Be careful not to add to the waistline measurement when you make this correction. The dotted lines represent your new cutting lines. Make the same correction on both front and back.

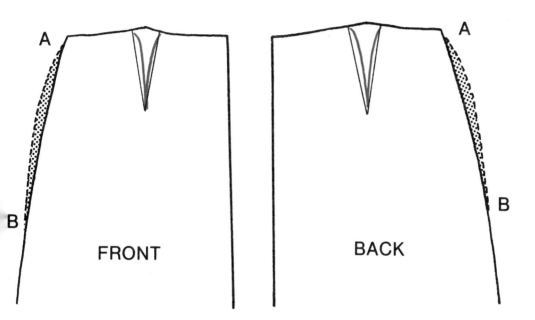

The area to be added is shown by shading. New dart lines are shown in red.

SEWING SOLUTION   Darts that pucker at the end are too long. Darts that show horizontal wrinkles are too tight. For a puckered dart, simply shorten the point of the dart at least ½" and restitch, blending into the existing stitching line at the waist. For a dart that wrinkles, restitch the dart in a concave line as shown in the drawing. Rip out the old stitching line.

New dart lines are shown in red.

PATTERN SOLUTION   For a puckered dart, shorten the point of the dart at least ½″ and redraw, connecting points A and B. For a wrinkled dart, the best solution is to change the shape of the dart from straight to concave as indicated in the drawing.

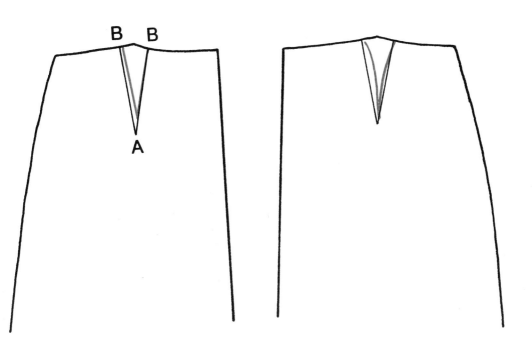

New dart lines are shown in red.

SEWING SOLUTION   *Please note:* A skirt that cups under the seat is so very tight that it is difficult to correct. The procedure outlined below will help the problem, but in all likelihood will not eliminate it unless your skirt has unusually large seam allowances.

Let out the side seams from the waistband to the hem as much as possible. Resew the darts in a concave shape. If the closure is in the front, let out the entire center back seam. If the skirt has a back zipper, let out the back seam from directly under the zipper all the way down to the hem.

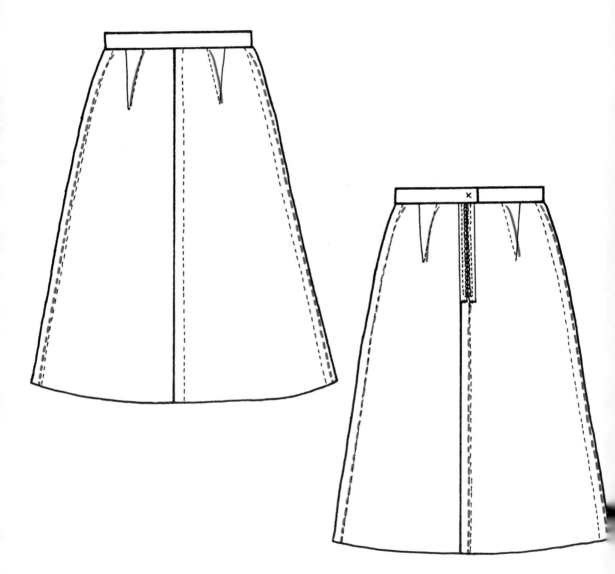

The old stitching line is shown in black, the new stitching line and new dart lines are shown in red.

PATTERN SOLUTION   Slash the pattern from point A to point B, and through the dart center from point C to point D. Arrange the pattern pieces as shown. Tape in place over a piece of tissue paper. The shaded area represents the amount of room you have gained. Shorten your darts ½″ and redraw them in a concave shape as shown. True the pattern lines at the side seam and hem.

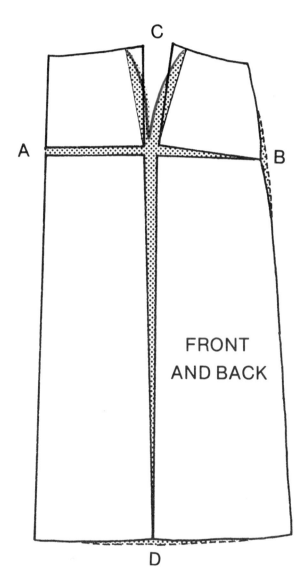

The area to be added is shown by shading. New dart lines are shown in red.

Bodices

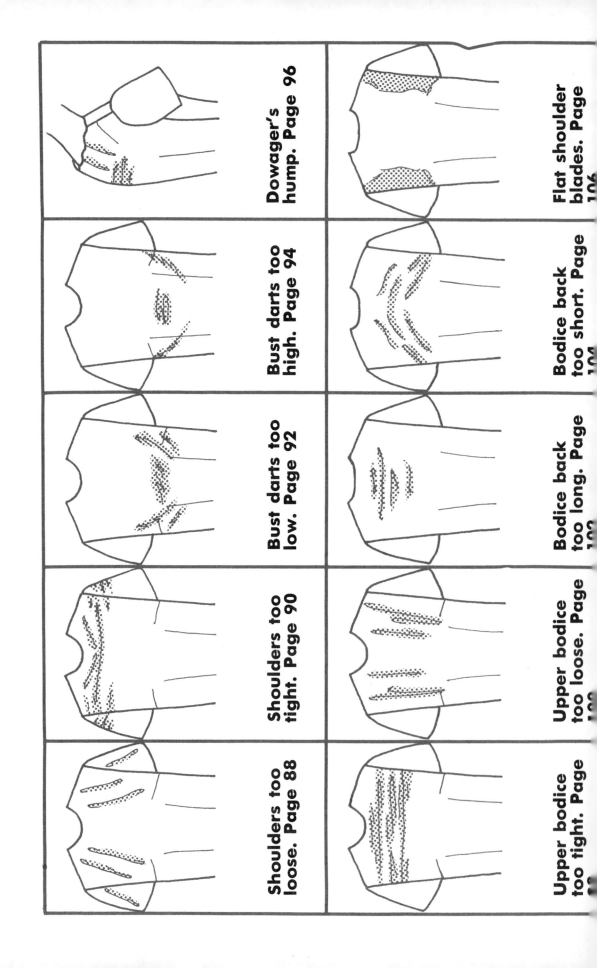

Dowager's hump. Page 96

Flat shoulder blades. Page 106

Bust darts too high. Page 94

Bodice back too short. Page 104

Bust darts too low. Page 92

Bodice back too long. Page 102

Shoulders too tight. Page 90

Upper bodice too loose. Page 100

Shoulders too loose. Page 88

Upper bodice too tight. Page 98

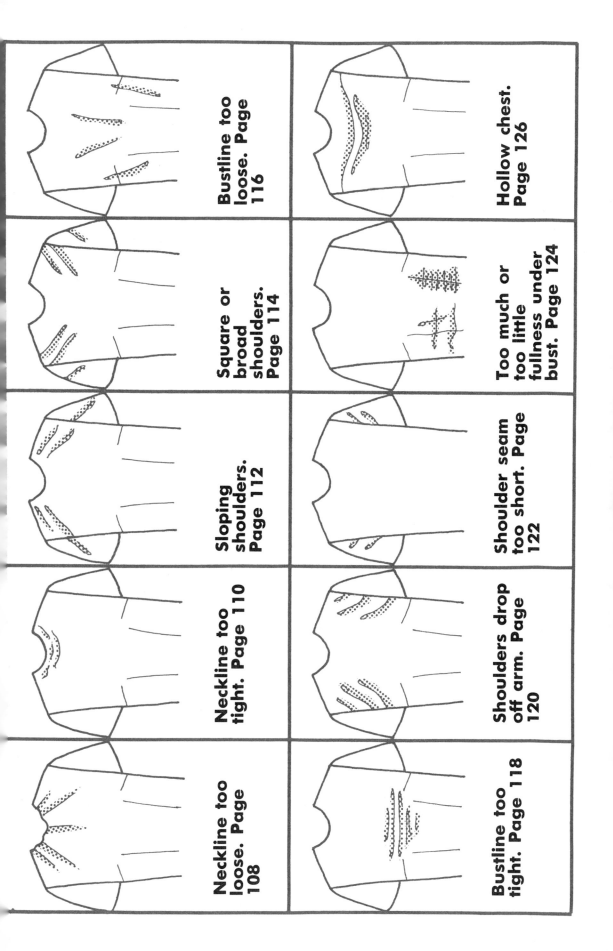

Bustline too loose. Page 116

Hollow chest. Page 126

Square or broad shoulders. Page 114

Too much or too little fullness under bust. Page 124

Sloping shoulders. Page 112

Shoulder seam too short. Page 122

Neckline too tight. Page 110

Shoulders drop off arm. Page 120

Neckline too loose. Page 108

Bustline too tight. Page 118

SEWING SOLUTION   Vertical droops through the upper bodice are an indication of a shoulder that is too loose. The problem can occur if you have very thin arms or if you tend to hunch your shoulders forward. Rip out the sleeves (if the garment has sleeves). Restitch the shoulder seam as shown, from point A to point B. Using your fashion curve, lower the armhole the same amount as you took up in the shoulder seam. Repin your sleeve. If you now have excess ease in the sleeve cap, trim off the sleeve cap as shown, between points C and D, until you achieve a good sleeve fit. Restitch the sleeve.

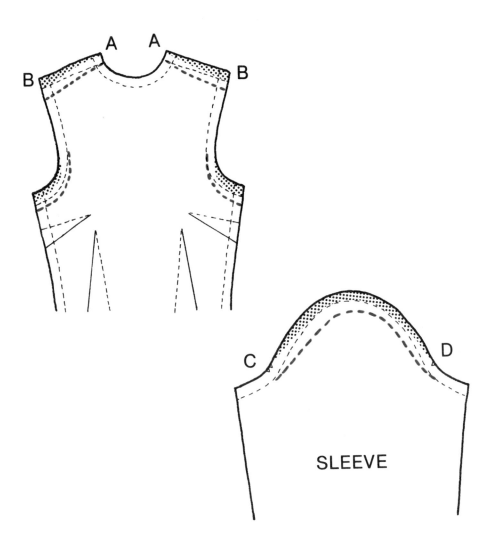

SLEEVE

The old stitching line is shown in black, the new stitching line is shown in red. Material to be trimmed off is shown by shading.

PATTERN SOLUTION   Slash the pattern from point A to point B, and overlap the amount of correction needed. Lower the armhole by the same amount, using your fashion curve to redraw the armhole. Measure the corrected armhole. If the measurement is the same as before the correction you do not have to correct your sleeve. If the armhole ends up being smaller, you must take enough ease out of the sleeve from point C to point D to maintain a good sleeve fit. *Please note:* Even if you don't correct the shoulder on both the front and back, you must lower the armhole to match the front or back you corrected.

The area to be cut off is shown by red lines, the area to be overlapped is shown by gray shading.

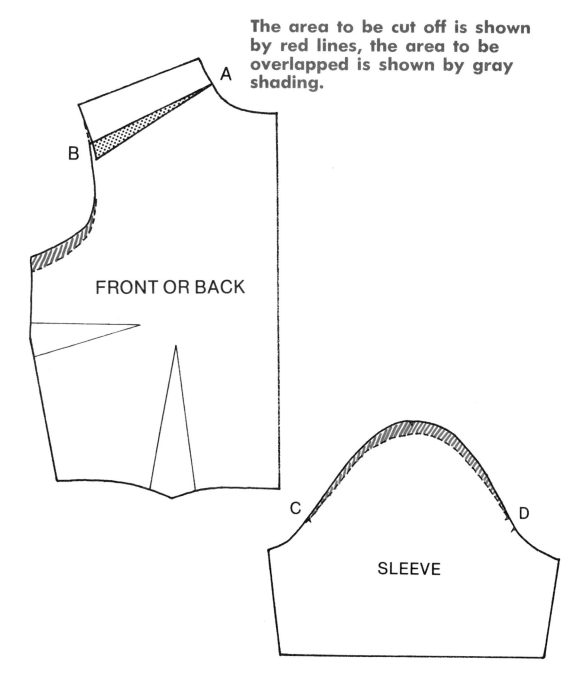

SEWING SOLUTION   Horizontal pulls between the upper armhole and across the sleeves are an indication of a shoulder that is too tight. This problem is usually caused by heavy upper arms. Rip out the sleeves (if the garment has sleeves). Let out the shoulder seams from point A to point B as much as possible. As this will make the armhole bigger, you need to let out the sleeve from point C to point D an equal amount so that the sleeve will still fit the armhole. Repin the sleeve and check to make sure it hangs properly. Restitch the sleeve.

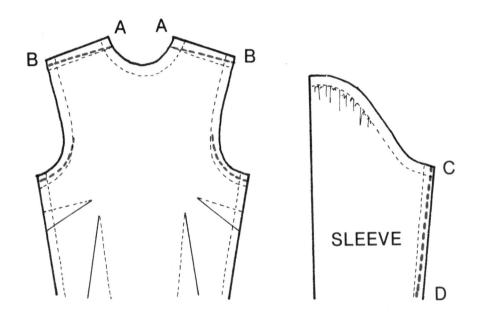

The old stitching line is shown in black, the new stitching line is shown in red.

PATTERN SOLUTION   Slash the pattern from point A to point B and spread the amount of correction needed. Raise the armhole by the same amount, using your fashion curve to redraw the armhole. Measure the corrected armhole. If the measurement is the same as before the correction you do not need to correct your sleeve pattern. If the armhole is larger you must add enough ease to the sleeve from point C to point D to maintain a good armhole fit. The dotted line is your new cutting line.

The area to be added is shown by gray shading.

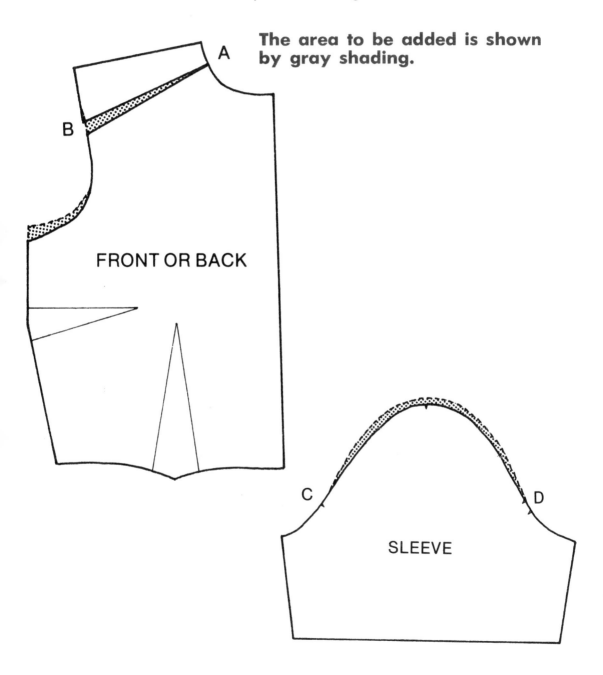

FRONT OR BACK

SLEEVE

SEWING SOLUTION   If you are high-busted, the points of your darts, whether regular darts or french darts, will generally be too low. This problem produces ripply diagonal sags in the area of the bustline. For regular darts, extend the point of the dart as much as necessary and restitch as shown below. For french darts, rip out the entire dart on both sides. Put the garment on inside out. Repin the dart, raising the point as needed, and taking up the fullness of the darts in a smooth line down to the side seam. Mark the darts with tailors' chalk. Take off the garment and restitch the darts.

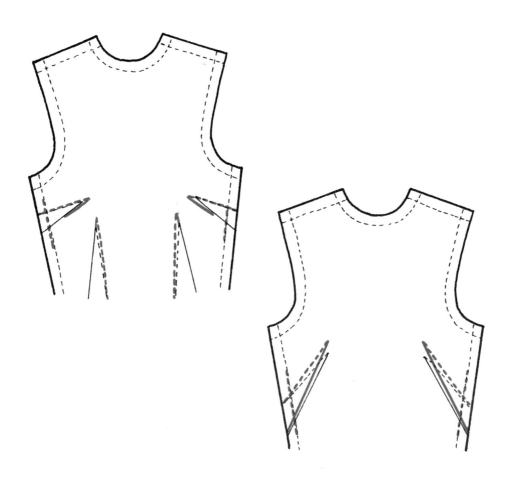

The old stitching line is shown in black, the new stitching line and new dart lines are shown in red.

PATTERN SOLUTION   For regular darts, determine how much you need to extend the dart points. Mark this on your pattern, approximately point A. Redraw the dart, connecting point A and point B. For french darts, determine how much you need to raise the bust point so that it will point to the apex, or center, of the bust. Mark this point A. Connect point A with point B at the side seam. Tape a piece of tissue to the bottom of the french dart. Fold the dart in, aiming the fold toward the waistline. Cut along the side seam, keeping the dart folded. Unfold the pattern. This procedure gives you the correct shape for the bottom of the dart.

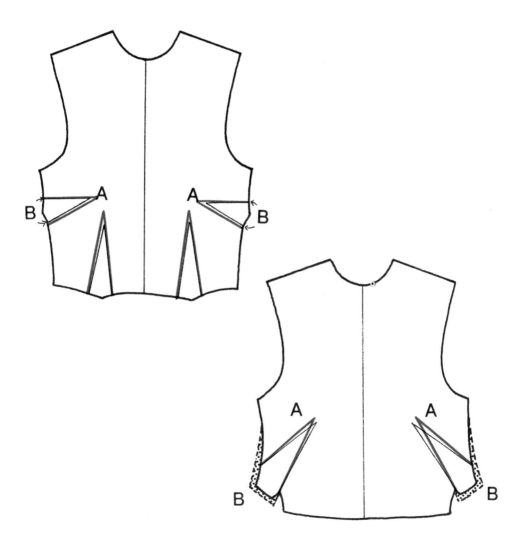

**New dart lines are shown in red.
The area to be added is shown
by shading.**

SEWING SOLUTION   If you have a heavy, full bustline, the points of your darts, whether regular or french, will generally be too high. Dart points that are too high have the effect of flattening the bust and creating uncomfortable, tight, horizontal pulls in the area of the bust darts. For regular darts, lower the point of the dart as much as necessary and restitch as shown below. Rip out the old stitching line where necessary. For french darts, rip out the entire dart on both sides. Put the garment on inside out. Repin the dart, lowering the point as needed, and taking up the fullness of the dart in a smooth line down to the side seam. Mark the darts with tailors' chalk. Remove the garment and restitch the darts.

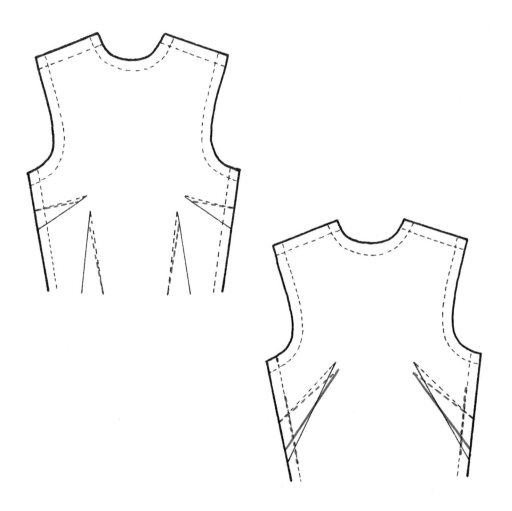

The old stitching line is shown in black, the new stitching line and new dart lines are shown in red.

PATTERN SOLUTION   For regular darts, determine how much you need to lower the dart points. Mark this on your pattern, approximately point A. Redraw the dart, connecting point A and point B. For french darts, determine how much you need to lower the bust point so that it will point to the apex, or center, of the bust. Mark this point A. Connect point A with point B at the side seam. Tape a piece of tissue to the bottom of the dart. Fold the dart in, aiming the fold toward the waistline. Cut along the side seam, keeping the dart folded. Unfold the pattern. This procedure gives you the correct shape for the bottom of the dart.

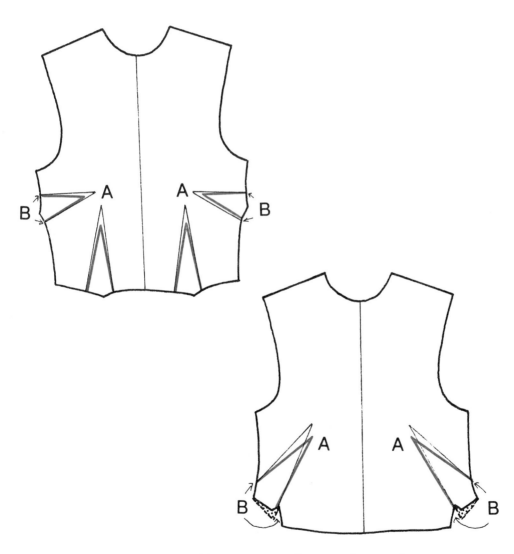

**New dart lines are shown in red.
The area to be added is shown
by shading.**

SEWING SOLUTION   If you have a dowager's hump, this will cause your garments to pull across the most prominent area of the hump, and stand away from your neck. Rip off the collar, if the garment has a collar. If the garment has a center back seam, let it out as much as possible in the most prominent area of the hump, blending your new stitching line smoothly into the old. Put the garment on inside out, and pin two small darts in the neckline to shape out any fullness there. Take off the garment. Mark the darts with tailors' chalk. Whatever is taken up in the two darts must be taken off the length of the collar so that the collar will still fit the neckline. Turn the collar inside out. Keeping the original shape of the collar as much as possible, trim off the amount needed for correction. Reset the collar.

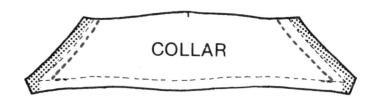

The old stitching line is shown in black, the new stitching line is shown in red. Material to be cut off is shown by gray shading.

PATTERN SOLUTION   Trace the neckline onto a piece of cardboard and cut out. Slash the pattern from point A to point C, and from point D to point B. Tape in place over a piece of tissue paper as shown. Redraw the original neckline using your cardboard cutout. The slightly curved center back seam that results will make your garment fit more smoothly. Determine the amount you need to take in at the neck to eliminate fullness. Put this amount into a neckline dart as shown below. The collar must be shortened by this same amount. For example, if you put two ⅜" darts in the back neckline, you must shorten your collar by ¾". Be careful to maintain the original shape of the collar as you shorten it.

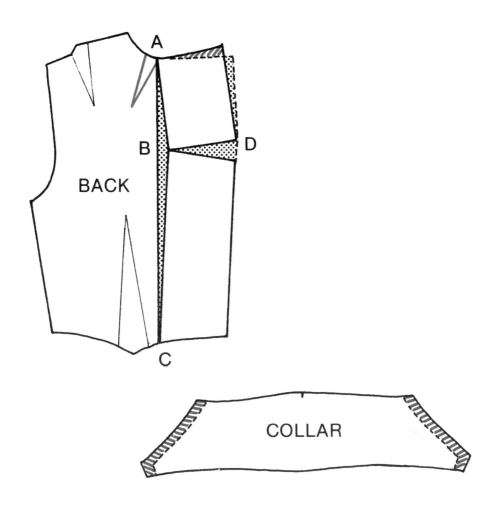

**The area to be cut off is shown
by red lines. The area to be
added is shown by gray shading.
New dart lines are shown in red.**

SEWING SOLUTION   If you have extremely broad shoulders you will get tight, uncomfortable horizontal pulls between your armholes. Let out the sleeve as much as possible between points A and B. Make the correction in both front and back if needed. If the garment has a center back seam and you are making the correction in the back, let out the seam from point C, under the collar, to point D.

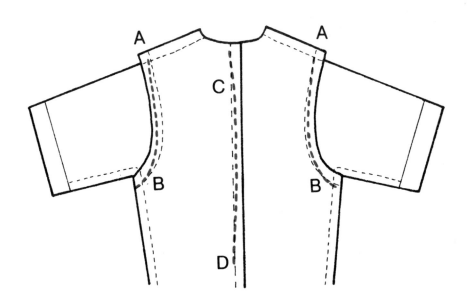

The old stitching line is shown in black, the new stitching line is shown in red.

PATTERN SOLUTION   Slash the pattern from point A to point B. Slash from point C to point D. Arrange the pattern pieces as shown and tape in place over a piece of tissue paper. The shaded area represents the amount of room you have gained without changing the other measurements of your pattern.

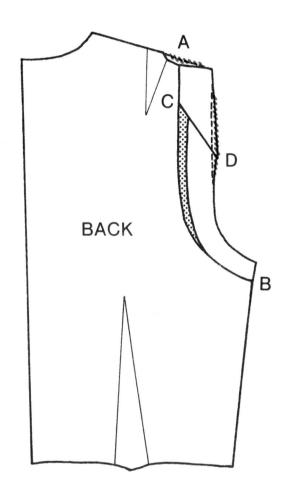

The area to be cut off is shown by red lines. The area to be added is shown by gray shading.

SEWING SOLUTION   If you have very narrow shoulders, your bodice
will fall in vertical sags between your armholes. If the garment has sleeves, rip
them out. Trim the armhole from back to front as shown below, being careful
to maintain as closely as possible the shape of the original armhole. Repin the
sleeve. If the armhole is too big for the sleeve after being trimmed, take up the
amount of correction needed on the side seam, and stitch down to nothing at
the waist. Reset the sleeves.

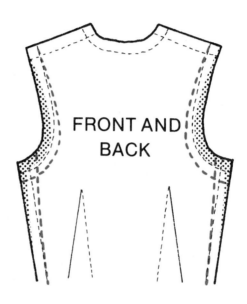

FRONT AND BACK

The old stitching line is shown in black, the new stitching line is shown in red. Material to be trimmed off is shown by shading.

PATTERN SOLUTION   Slash the pattern from point A to point B, being careful not to interfere with the shoulder dart if you are making the correction in the back. Overlap the amount of correction needed and tape in new position. True the shoulder line to match the side not being corrected. If you make the correction both front and back, be sure to overlap the same amount so that your shoulder seams still match.

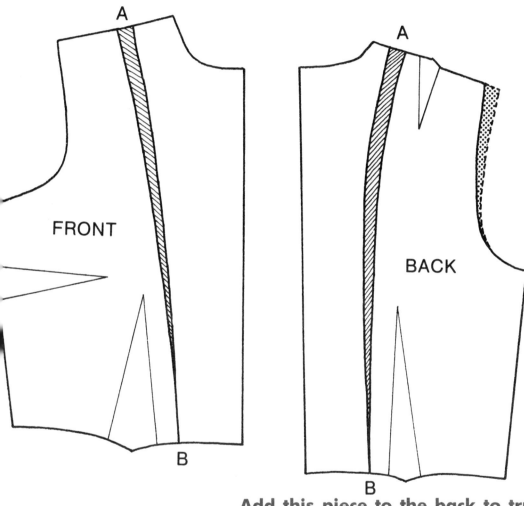

FRONT

BACK

Add this piece to the back to true the shoulder seam if the overlap correction is made only on the front. Add the piece to the front if the overlap correction is made only on the back.

The area to be overlapped is shown by black lines. The area to be added is shown by gray shading.

SEWING SOLUTION   If you have very erect posture you may get horizontal folds between your shoulder blades. This is rather difficult to correct in a finished garment. The easiest solution is to fold the excess fabric up into a tuck from shoulder to shoulder. Stitch the tuck from the inside, and then topstitch on the outside. This creates the effect of a yoke across the back. If you don't want a yoke, you must rip the collar, neckline facings if any, and the shoulder seams from the neck to about 1″ from the sleeve. Trace the shape of the back neckline onto cardboard and cut out. Put the garment on inside out and lift the shoulders until the sags disappear, and pin in new position. Take off the garment and recut neckline using cardboard cutout as a guide. Trim excess fabric from the back. Restitch the shoulder seams and reset the collar and neckline facings.

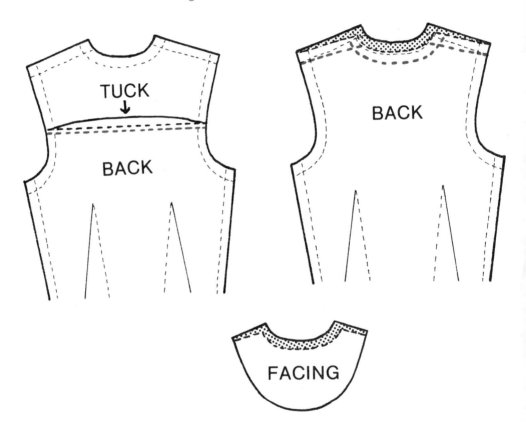

The old stitching line is shown in black, the new stitching line is shown in red. Material to be trimmed off is shown by shading. Top stitching is shown by a heavy black broken line.

PATTERN SOLUTION   Slash the pattern from point A to point C, through the point of the dart. Slash from point B to point D through the center of the dart. Overlap the amount of correction needed. Notice that you are closing up your shoulder dart and making it smaller. Tape the pattern in this new position. True pattern edges where necessary.

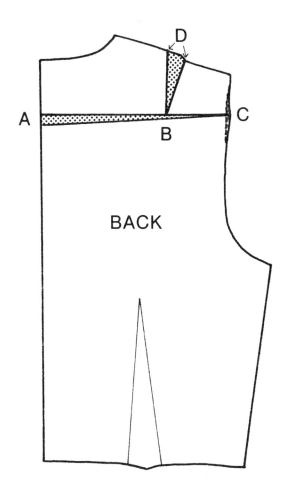

The area to be overlapped is shown by gray shading. The area to be cut off is shown by red lines.

SEWING SOLUTION   If you have a sloping back and rounded shoulders, these tend to pull the bodice back up, creating diagonal pulls across the upper bodice. *Please note:* This is impossible to correct in a finished garment as you need more fabric through the length of the center back, and you have no extra fabric.

PATTERN SOLUTION   Slash the pattern from point A to point C, and from point B to point D. Arrange the pattern pieces as shown, spreading the center back seam as much as needed for a smooth fit. Notice that you are opening up your shoulder dart and giving it more shape. Tape the pattern pieces in the new position over a piece of tissue paper. The shaded area shows the amount you have gained.

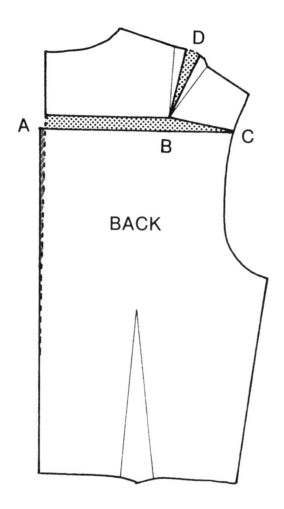

The area to be cut off is shown by red lines. The area to be added is shown by gray shading.

SEWING SOLUTION   Vertical droops at the outside of the shoulder are an indication of too much fabric in the armhole. This can be caused by flat shoulder blades in back or a hollow between the bust and the armpit in front. Rip the sleeves (if the garment has sleeves). Put the garment on inside out. For the back correction, pin a small dart, as shown in the drawing, taking up as much fullness as necessary to achieve a smooth armhole fit. Repin the sleeve and determine how much ease you need to take out of the sleeve cap so as to make the sleeve fit the smaller armhole created by the new dart. Mark the dart and the sleeve with tailors' chalk. Take off the garment. Trim the sleeve cap as necessary. Stitch the new darts, and reset the sleeves. Make the same correction for the front if necessary, but angle the point of the dart down toward the apex of the bust as shown in drawing.

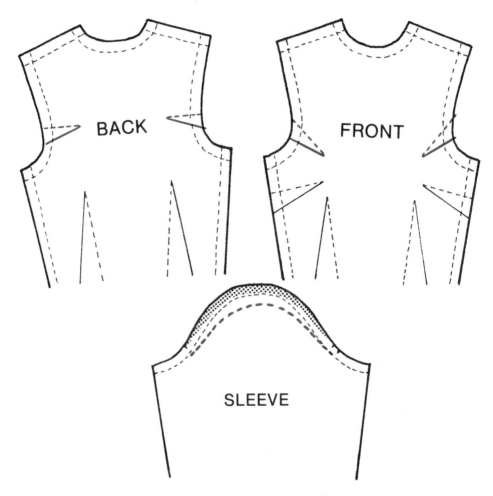

BACK   FRONT

SLEEVE

The old stitching line is shown in black, the new stitching lines and new dart lines are shown in red. Material to be trimmed off is shown by gray shading.

PATTERN SOLUTION   Slash the pattern from the point where the fullness gaps the most, point A to point B. For the back you will be slashing to the point of the shoulder dart; for the front you will be slashing to the point of the side bust dart. Slash through the center of the shoulder dart in back to point B or through the center of the side bust dart in front. Overlap the slash along long A–B, taking up as much fullness as you need to eliminate the gap. Notice as you do this that you are opening up the shoulder dart or the side bust dart and making it larger. You are making the armhole smaller and must take off the length of the sleeve cap an amount equal to what you overlapped. Slash the sleeve from point C to point D and overlap the front or back or both, depending on where you made your bodice correction. Tape the patterns in their new positions.

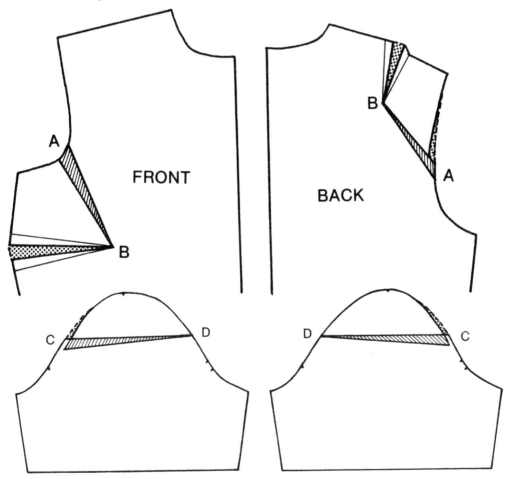

The area to be overlapped is shown by black lines, the area to be added is shown by gray shading.

SEWING SOLUTION   Diagonal droops that stand away from the body are an indication of a neckline that is too big. The easiest way to correct this is to add small neckline darts to take up the additional fullness. If the garment has a collar, rip it off. Put the garment on inside out. Pin in two small darts as shown, one on either side of the neck. Take off the garment and mark the darts with tailors' chalk. Turn the collar inside out. You must shorten the collar the same amount you took up in the darts, being careful to maintain the original shape of the collar as you trim it. Sew the darts, restitch the collar, and reset the collar. If you have a neckline facing, you must make the same dart correction in the facing as you made on the neckline.

The old stitching lines are shown in black, the new stitching lines and new dart lines are shown in red. Material to be trimmed off is shown by gray shading.

PATTERN SOLUTION   Slash from point A at the neckline down to point B, the point of the side bust dart. Slash through the center of the dart from point C to point B. Overlap the neckline the amount of correction needed, and tape the pattern in this new position. Notice that you are opening up the side bust dart and giving it more shape. Make an equal correction on the collar and the neck facing, if the garment has them.

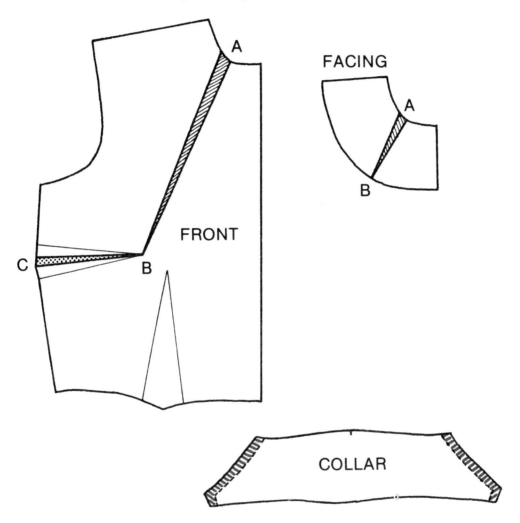

The area to be overlapped is shown by black lines, the area to be added is shown by gray shading. The area to be cut off is shown by red lines.

SEWING SOLUTION   Uncomfortable horizontal pulls at the neckline mean that the neck is too tight. Rip off the collar and/or neckline facing. Determine how much you need to lower the neckline to achieve a comfortable fit and trim away the excess fabric as shown below. Trim the neckline facing by an equal amount. Turn the collar inside out and let out the seams as much as possible to compensate for the larger neckline. If you are making a big correction, you probably will not be able to let out the collar enough to make it fit the neckline as before, and the ends of the collar will sit further back from the center front seam than they did before the correction. Reset the collar and neckline facing.

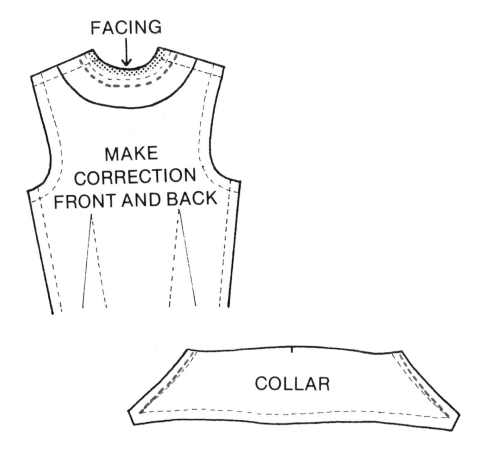

FACING

MAKE
CORRECTION
FRONT AND BACK

COLLAR

The old stitching line is shown in black, the new stitching line is shown in red. Material to be trimmed off is shown by shading.

PATTERN SOLUTION   Determine how much you need to lower the neckline to achieve a comfortable fit and trim off this amount both front and back, being careful to keep the shoulder seams the same length as you make the correction. Make the same correction on the front and back neck facings if the pattern has facings. Whatever you take off the top of the facing should be added to the bottom of the facing to maintain the original facing width. Measure the corrected neckline and determine how much you need to add to the length of the collar so that it will fit your corrected neckline. Add the necessary amount to the collar, being sure to maintain the shape of the original collar, as shown below.

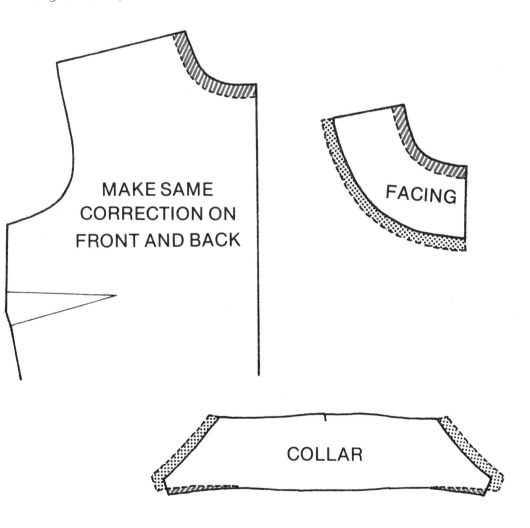

The area to be added is shown by gray shading, the area to be cut off is shown by red lines.

SEWING SOLUTION   Sloping shoulders will produce diagonal droops from the neckline to the shoulder. Rip out the sleeves from armseye to armseye. Put the garment on inside out. Pin up the shoulders as much as necessary at the outside edge, going up to nothing at the neckline. Take off the garment and mark the shoulder corrections with tailors' chalk. Repin the sleeves and determine how much you have to take off the ease of the sleeve cap to make the sleeve fit the new smaller armhole. Trim off this excess ease. Restitch the shoulder seams and reset the sleeves.

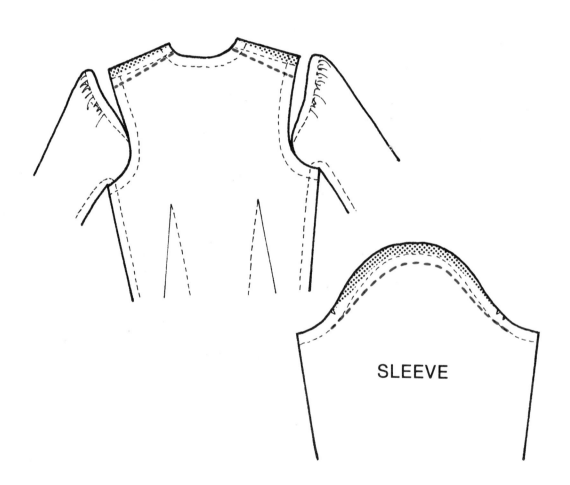

SLEEVE

The old stitching line is shown in black, the new stitching line is shown in red. Material to be trimmed off is shown by gray shading.

PATTERN SOLUTION   Determine how much you need to take off the outside shoulder edge to eliminate your sags and mark this approximately point A on the pattern. Using a ruler, connect this with point B at the neckline. Whatever you take off the length of the armhole must be taken from the sleeve in equal amount to maintain good sleeve fit. Slash the sleeve from point C to point D and overlap the amount of correction. Tape the sleeve in the new position.

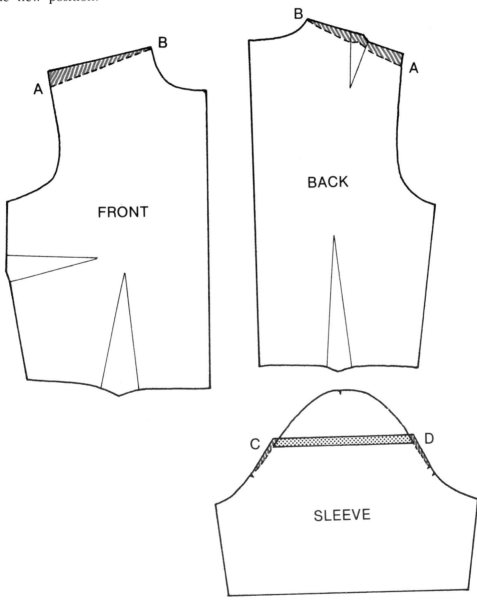

The area to be cut off is shown by red lines. The area to be overlapped is shown by gray shading.

SEWING SOLUTION   Square or broad shoulders will often produce diagonal pulls from the shoulders to the center of the garment. If the garment has sleeves, rip them out. Rip the shoulder seams up to about 1″ from the collar. Put the garment on inside out. Repin the shoulder seams, letting out enough to eliminate the wrinkles. Let out the underarm seam from point A down to nothing at point B, to compensate for the armhole being made larger by letting out the shoulder seam. Take off the garment and restitch the shoulder seams, blending the new stitching line smoothly into the old one. Repin the sleeve. If it is too small for the armhole, pull some of the ease stitches out of the sleeve until it fits the armhole well. Restitch the sleeves.

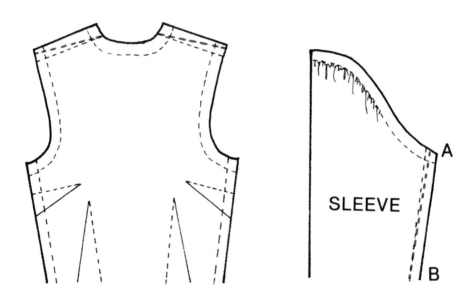

The old stitching line is shown in black, the new stitching line is shown in red.

PATTERN SOLUTION   Determine how much you need to add to the outside shoulder and mark this point A on the pattern. Using a ruler, connect this with point B at the neckline. Whatever you add to the length of the armhole must be added to the sleeve in equal amount in order to maintain good sleeve fit. Slash the sleeve from point C to point D and spread the amount of correction. Tape the sleeve in the new position over a piece of tissue paper.

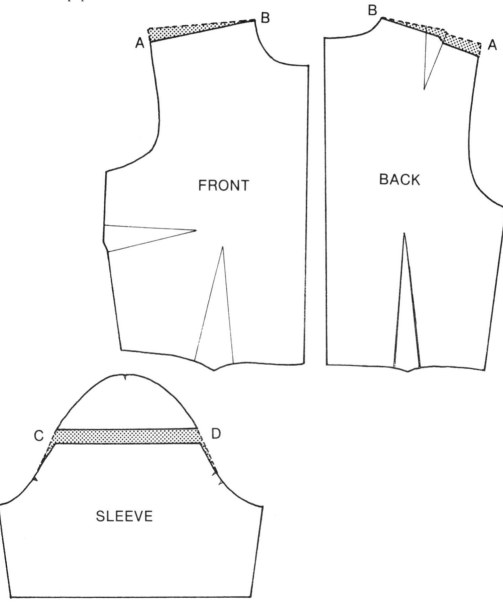

The area to be added is shown by gray shading.

SEWING SOLUTION   If you have a small bust, you may get loose vertical droops across the front of your garment. If you have a narrow back, you may get the same problem in the back of your garment. Put the garment on inside out. Pin up the side seams as much as necessary to eliminate the droops. Pin up the waistline bust darts in a convex shape. Take off the garment. Mark your side seam and bust dart corrections with tailors' chalk. Stitch the side seams up from point A to point B as shown in the drawing. Restitch your darts.

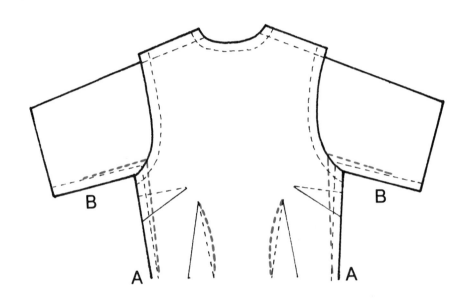

The old stitching line is shown in black, the new stitching line is shown in red.

PATTERN SOLUTION   Slash the pattern from point A to point B, through the point of the side bust dart. Slash the pattern from point C to point D, through the point of the waistline bust dart. Overlap the amount of correction needed and tape pattern in new position. True the edges of the pattern if necessary. Relocate points of bust darts and connect with original dart lines at waistline and side seam. This correction will make both the bodice and the darts smaller. Make the correction on both front and back only if needed.

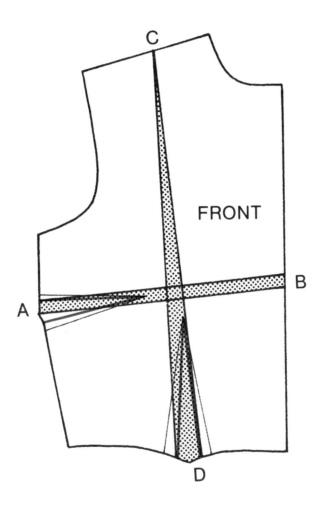

The area to be overlapped is shown by gray shading. New dart lines are shown in red.

SEWING SOLUTION   If you have a large, full bust or prominent shoulder blades, you will often get tight, horizontal pulls across the bust or between the shoulder blades. Rip the side seams from point A to point B. Put the garment on inside out. Pin up the side seams, letting out as much as necessary to eliminate the wrinkles. If the bodice still pulls, let out the armhole seams between points C and D. Take off the garment and restitch the side seams and the armhole seams if necessary.

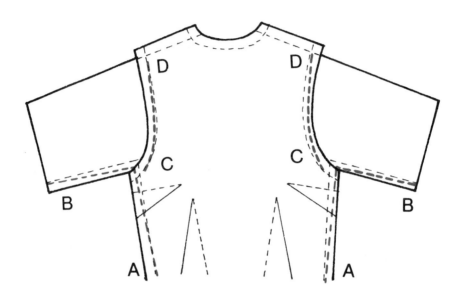

The old stitching line is shown in black, the new stitching line is shown in red.

PATTERN SOLUTION   Slash the pattern from point A to point B, through the point of the side bust dart. Slash the pattern from point C to point D, through the point of the waistline bust dart. Spread the pattern the amount of correction needed as shown below. Tape the pattern in the new position over a piece of tissue paper. True the edges of the pattern if necessary. Relocate points of bust darts and connect with original dart lines at waistline and side seam. This correction will make both the bodice and the darts larger.

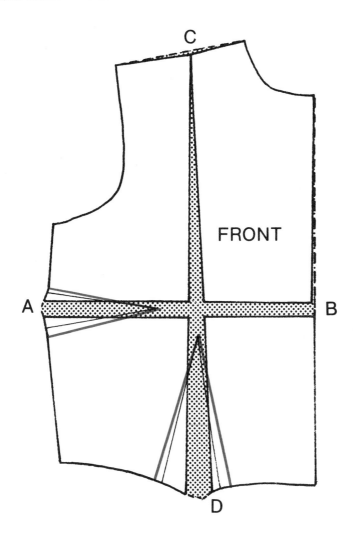

The area to be added is shown by gray shading. New dart lines are shown in red.

SEWING SOLUTION   If you have narrow shoulders, your shoulder seams may drop off the top of your arms. If the garment has sleeves, rip them from armseye to armseye. Try on the garment right side out, and repin the sleeves in the correct position, so that the shoulder seam will sit directly over the acromion, the knobby bone at the end of the shoulder. Mark the new seam line with tailors' chalk. Take off the garment and restitch the sleeves. Trim off the excess seam allowance.

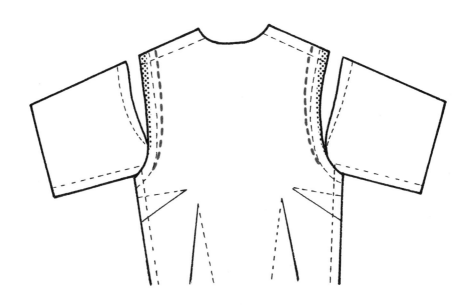

The old stitching line is shown in black, the new stitching line is shown in red. Material to be trimmed off is shown by gray shading.

PATTERN SOLUTION   Determine the amount you need to take off the armhole to put the shoulder seam in the correct position directly over the acromion, the knobby bone at the end of the shoulder. Mark this approximately point A. Using your fashion curve, redraw the armhole, blending your line into the armhole around point B. The dotted line is your new cutting line.

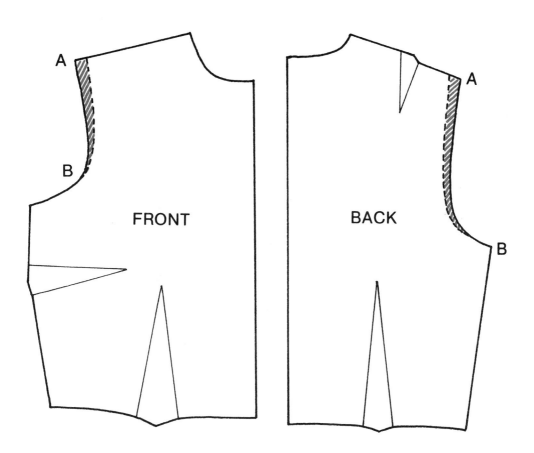

The area to be cut off is shown by red lines.

SEWING SOLUTION   If you have broad shoulders, your shoulder seams may be too short, which will cause your sleeves to pull up uncomfortably. If the garment has sleeves, rip them from armseye to armseye. Put the garment on right side out, and repin the sleeves in the correct position. The shoulder seam should sit directly over the acromion, the knobby bone at the end of the shoulder. Mark the new seam with tailors' chalk. Take off the garment and restitch the sleeves. *Please note:* You can make this correction only if you have sufficient seam allowance in the armhole and the sleeve.

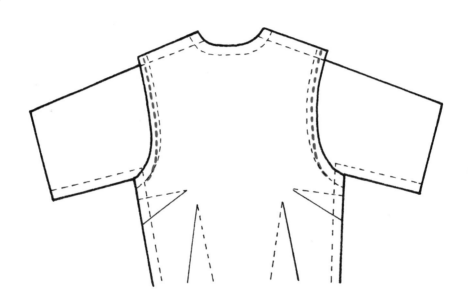

The old stitching line is shown in black, the new stitching line is shown in red.

PATTERN SOLUTION   Determine the amount you need to add to the armhole to put the shoulder seam in the correct position over the acromion, the knobby bone at the end of the shoulder. Mark this approximately point A. Using your fashion curve, redraw the armhole, blending your line into the armhole around point B. The dotted line is your new cutting line.

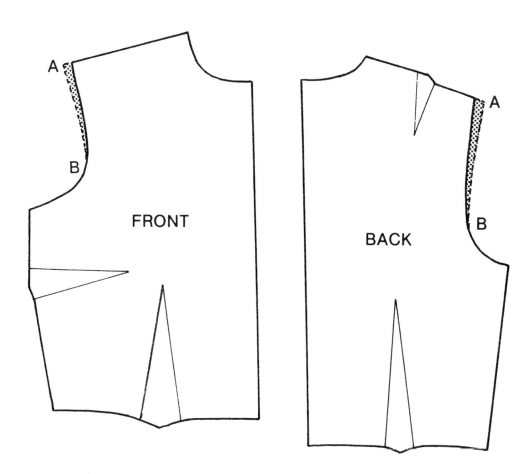

The area to be added is shown by gray shading.

SEWING SOLUTION   If you have a thin rib cage, you will have a lot of extra fullness under your bust. If you have a heavy rib cage, the area under the bust will pull and feel tight. To eliminate extra fullness, sew your bust darts in a convex shape as shown in the drawing, taking up as much as you need to achieve a smooth fit. You may also need to take up the side seams from point A to point B if the correction is a large one. If you need more room under the bust, rip out the darts and restitch them in a concave shape as shown below. If this correction does not give you sufficient ease, let out the side seams from point C to point D. Balance your correction between the side seams and the darts.

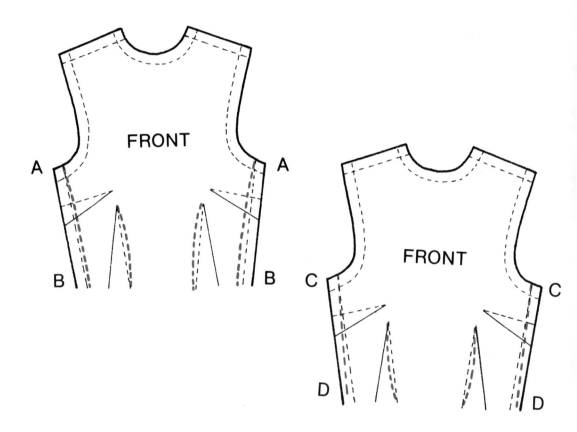

The old stitching line is shown in black, the new stitching line is shown in red.

PATTERN SOLUTION   For a thin rib cage, draw your darts in a convex shape. If necessary, pare down the side seam from point A to point B. For a heavy rib cage, redraw your darts in a concave shape. Add to the side seams from point C to point D if you need additional room. The dotted lines represent your new cutting lines.

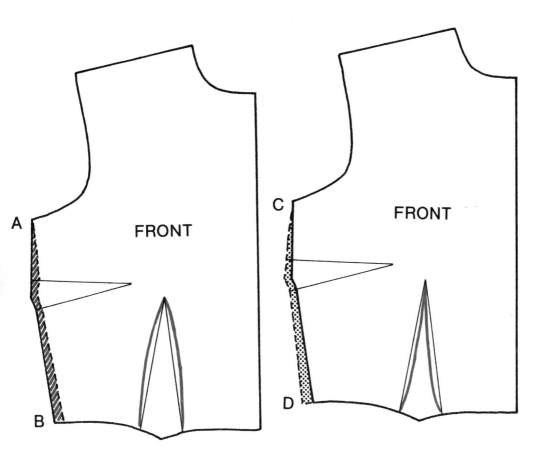

The area to be cut off is shown by red lines, the area to be added is shown by gray shading. New dart lines are shown in red.

SEWING SOLUTION   If you have a hollow chest, you will get horizontal folds above the bustline between the armholes. Rip the collar and/or neck facings. Rip the shoulder seams from the neck to about 1″ from the sleeve. Trace the shape of the front neckline onto cardboard and cut out. Put the garment on inside out. Pull up the front of the garment at the neck edge of the shoulder until the sags disappear and pin in place. Take off garment and recut neckline using cardboard cutout as a guide. Cut front neck facing to match. Restitch the shoulder seams. Reset the collar and/or neckline facing.

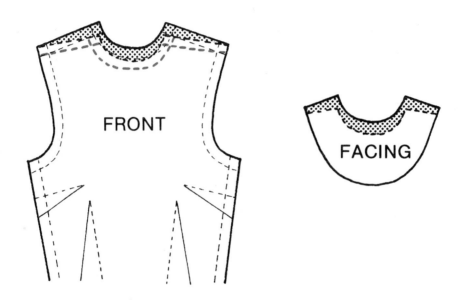

The old stitching line is shown in black, the new stitching line is shown in red. Material to be trimmed off is shown by gray shading.

PATTERN SOLUTION   Trace the top of the pattern on cardboard, mark the notches and the grainline, and cut out. Slash the pattern from point A to point B and overlap the amount of correction needed. Tape the pattern in this new position. Put your cardboard cutout on the bodice pattern, lining up notches and the grainline. Tape a piece of tissue under the shoulder and the armhole. Trim the center front and the neckline where they extend beyond the cardboard cutout. Trace the new shoulder line and armhole from the cardboard cutout onto the piece of tissue you taped on the corrected pattern. The dotted lines represents the new cutting line.

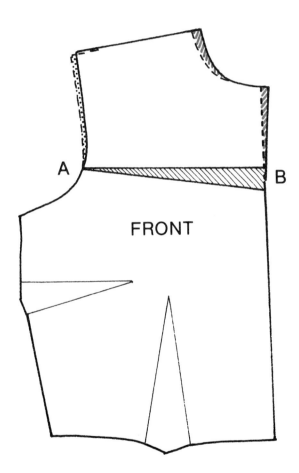

The area to be overlapped is shown by black lines, the area to be added is shown by gray shading. The area to be cut off is shown by red lines.

Armholes and Sleeves

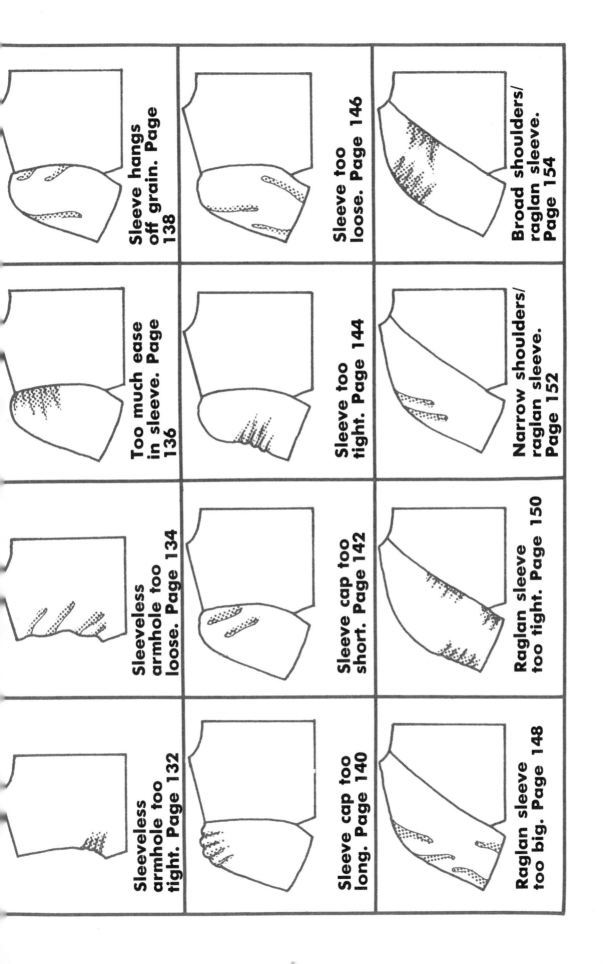

Sleeveless armhole too tight. Page 132

Sleeveless armhole too loose. Page 134

Too much ease in sleeve. Page 136

Sleeve hangs off grain. Page 138

Sleeve cap too long. Page 140

Sleeve cap too short. Page 142

Sleeve too tight. Page 144

Sleeve too loose. Page 146

Raglan sleeve too big. Page 148

Raglan sleeve too tight. Page 150

Narrow shoulders/ raglan sleeve. Page 152

Broad shoulders/ raglan sleeve. Page 154

SEWING SOLUTION   If your sleeveless armhole is too small you will get tight, uncomfortable horizontal pulls in the area of the armseye. Rip the sleeve facing. Trim the armhole down until it feels comfortable when the garment is on. Trim the armhole facings down to match. If you do not have a big enough facing to do this, you may finish the armhole with bias tape. Restitch the facings.

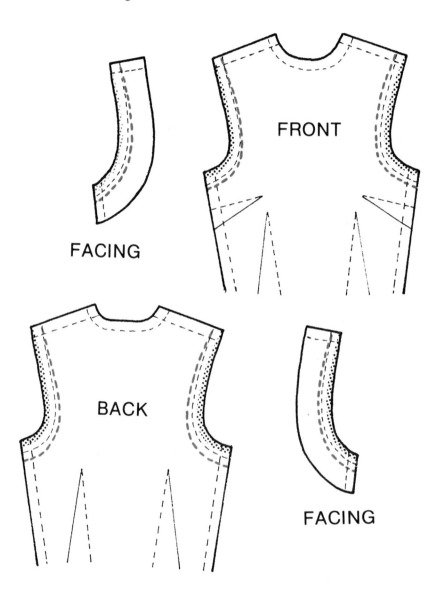

FACING

FRONT

BACK

FACING

The old stitching line is shown in black, the new stitching line is shown in red. Material to be trimmed off is shown by gray shading.

PATTERN SOLUTION   Determine how much you need to lower and enlarge the armhole to achieve a comfortable fit. Use your fashion curve to redraw the armhole in the new location. Make the same correction on the armhole facings. The dotted lines represent your new cutting lines.

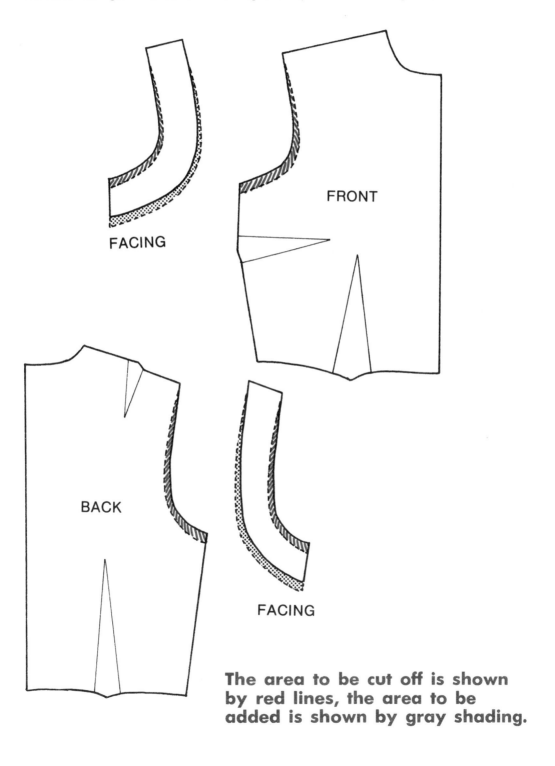

FACING

FRONT

BACK

FACING

The area to be cut off is shown by red lines, the area to be added is shown by gray shading.

SEWING SOLUTION   A sleeveless armhole that is too big will produce loose, droopy, diagonal folds falling from the armhole to the chest area. Rip the sleeve facing. Put the garment on inside out. Pin up the shoulder seams and the side seams until you achieve a smooth, comfortable fit. Mark the corrections with tailors' chalk, and make an equal correction on the armhole facings. Take off the garment. Resew the shoulder and side seams. Reset the armhole facings.

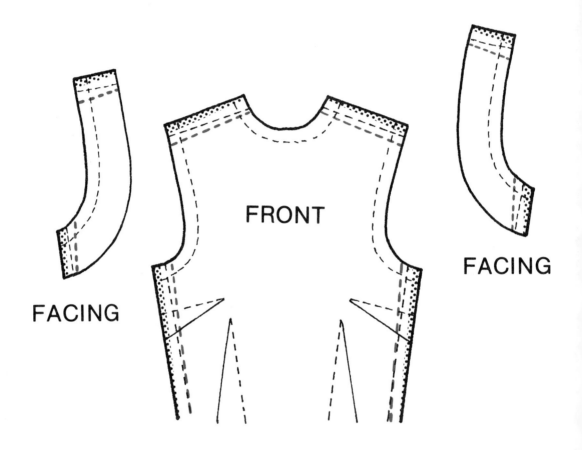

FRONT

FACING

FACING

The old stitching line is shown in black, the new stitching line is shown in red. Material to be trimmed off is shown by gray shading.

PATTERN SOLUTION   Determine how much you need to eliminate from the armhole to get a smooth sag-free fit. Divide this amount between the shoulder seam and the side seam. Mark these points A and C. Connect with points B and D. Make the same corrections on the armhole facings. The dotted lines are your new cutting lines. *Please note:* If the armhole is so big that it shows your bra, add to the armhole and facing between points E and C as shown on the front pattern below.

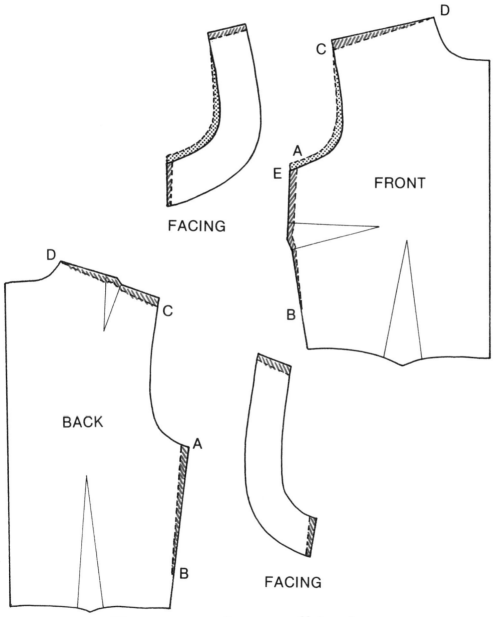

The area to be cut off is shown by red lines, the area to be added is shown by gray shading.

SEWING SOLUTION   Small puckers and gathers in a sleeve that's supposed to fit smoothly indicate that there is too much ease in the sleeve cap. Rip the sleeve from armseye to armseye. Run a line of gathering stitches below the original seamline as shown below. Pull up the stitches and pin the sleeve back into the armhole. If you still have puckers, try another line of stitches below the first one. Repeat this procedure until you have determined the proper stitching line. Trim the excess ease from the sleeve cap. Restitch the sleeves.

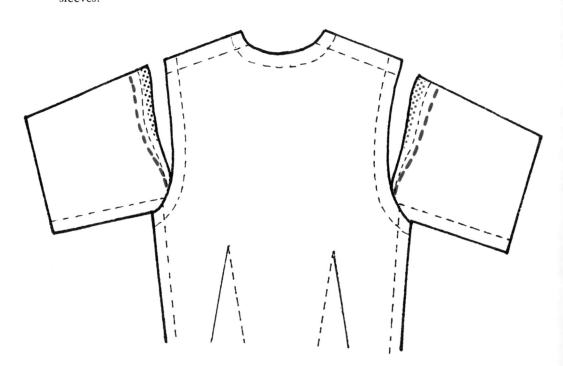

The old stitching line is shown in black, the new stitching line is shown in red. Material to be trimmed off is shown by gray shading.

PATTERN SOLUTION   Determine the amount of ease you need to remove from the sleeve cap to achieve a smooth pucker-free fit. Take this from the sleeve between point A and point B. The dotted line represents your new cutting line.

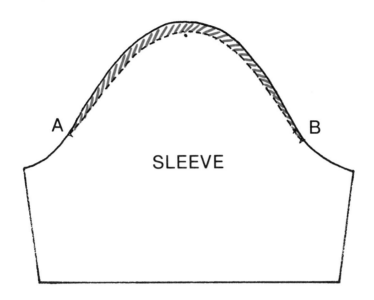

The area to be cut off is shown by red lines.

SEWING SOLUTION   A sleeve that hangs off-grain is the result of ease being poorly distributed through the armhole. Rip the sleeve from armseye to armseye. Rip the gathering stitches from the cap of the sleeve and press flat. Run two rows of gathering stitches along the cap between armseyes and shown below. Pull up the stitches and redistribute the ease around the armhole until the sleeve hangs properly. Reset the sleeves. *Please note:* If this does not correct your problem, it probably means the sleeves were cut off-grain at the factory and cannot be corrected.

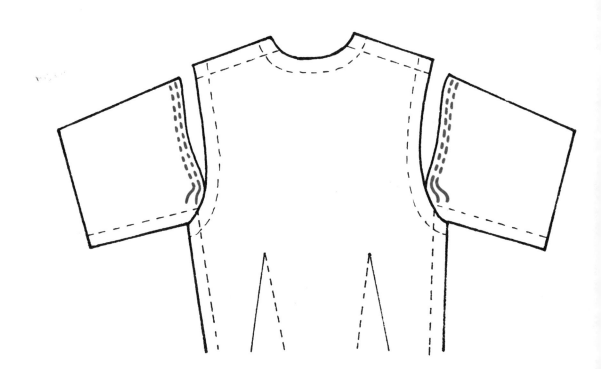

The stitching lines are shown in black, the gathering stitches are shown in red.

PATTERN SOLUTION   You do not need to make an actual pattern correction; just move the matching dot on the sleeve that corresponds with the shoulder seam. This problem only shows up once the garment has been made. If your sleeve hangs to the front, you must move your ease to the front, and move your matching dot to the back by an equal amount. If your sleeve hangs to the back, you must move your ease to the back and move your matching dot forward of its original position by an equal amount.

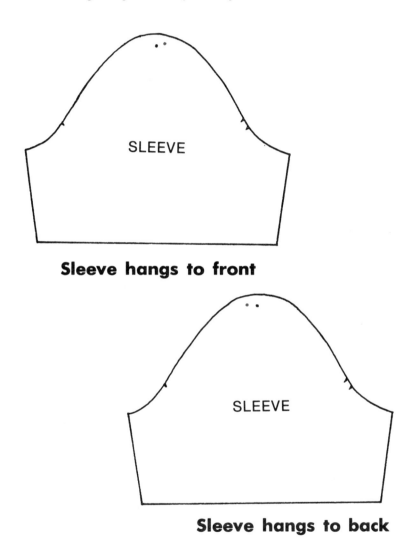

Sleeve hangs to front

Sleeve hangs to back

The old shoulder matching dot is shown in black, the new dot is shown in red.

SEWING SOLUTION   Ripply folds of cloth across the top of the arm indicate that your sleeve cap is too long. Rip the sleeve from armseye to armseye. Put the garment on inside out. Pull the center of the sleeve cap up until the ripples disappear. Pin sleeve in new position. Mark correction with tailors' chalk. Take off the garment and restitch the sleeves. Trim off excess seam allowance.

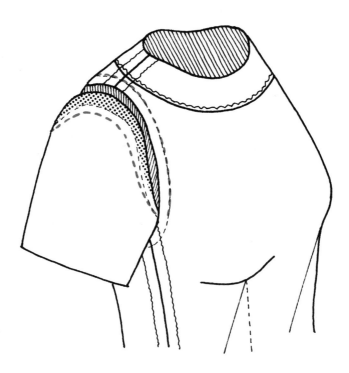

The old stitching line is shown in black, the new stitching line is shown in red. Material to be trimmed off is shown by gray shading.

PATTERN SOLUTION   Slash the pattern from point A to point B and overlap the amount of correction needed to eliminate the ripples in the cap. Tape the pattern in this new position. True the pattern edges if necessary.

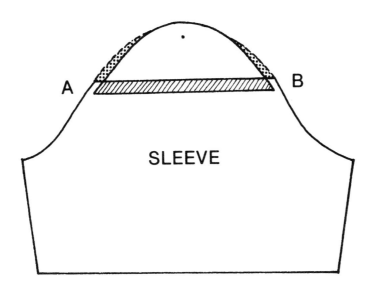

The area to be overlapped is shown by black lines, the area to be added is shown by gray shading.

SEWING SOLUTION   Diagonal pulls from the armseye to the top of the sleeve cap mean that your sleeve cap is too short. Rip the sleeves from armseye to armseye. Put the garment on inside out. Repin the sleeves, letting out enough to eliminate the wrinkles. If you don't have sufficient seam allowance to do this, try the following procedure: Rip the entire sleeve and rip the underarm sleeve seam. Trip the sleeve as shown below, which has the effect of making the sleeve cap longer. Pin the trimmed sleeve into the armhole to make sure you have a good fit. Restitch the underarm sleeve seam, and reset the sleeve.

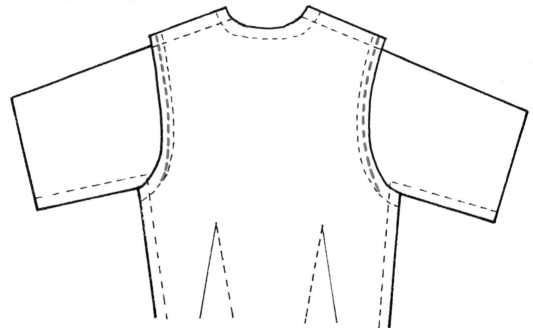

Make this correction from front to back.

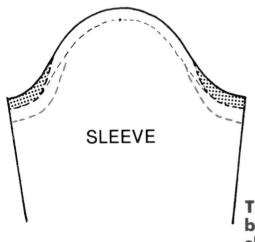

SLEEVE

The old stitching line is shown in black, the new stitching line is shown in red. Material to be trimmed off is shown by gray shading.

PATTERN SOLUTION   Slash the pattern from point A to point B and spread the amount of correction necessary to eliminate the wrinkles in the sleeve cap. Tape the pattern in this new position over a piece of tissue paper. True the pattern edges if necessary.

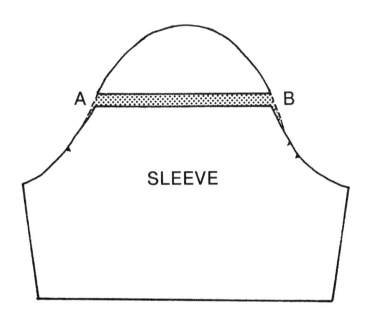

The area to be added is shown by gray shading.

SEWING SOLUTION   Tight horizontal pulls across the upper arm indicate your sleeve is too tight. Let out the sleeve as much as possible between points A and B in both the front and the back. Let out the underarm seam starting at point C and gradually tapering to nothing at point D.

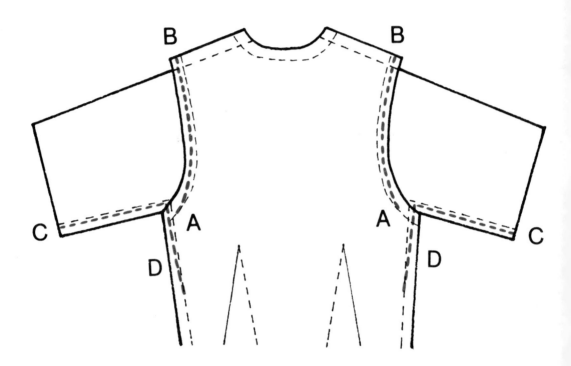

The old stitching line is shown in black, the new stitching line is shown in red.

PATTERN SOLUTION   Slash the pattern from point A to point B, and from point C to point D. Arrange the pieces, as shown, over a piece of tissue paper and tape in the new position. True the pattern edges if necessary. The shaded area shows the amount you have gained. Distribute the additional ease evenly from armseye to armseye when sewing from the corrected pattern.

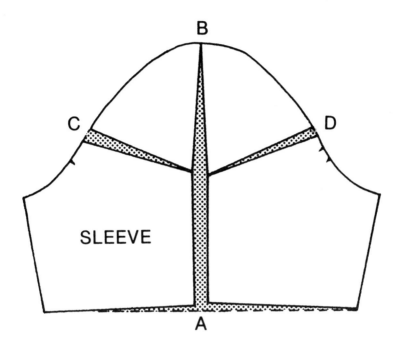

**The area to be added is shown
by gray shading.**

SEWING SOLUTION   If you have thin arms, your sleeve may droop unbecomingly, indicating too much fullness in the sleeve. Rip the sleeves from the garment and rip the underarm sleeve seams. Lay the sleeves flat, one on top of the other. Trim the sleeves as shown below. Notice that you are paring much more from the width of the sleeve cap than from the height of the sleeve cap. Resew the underarm sleeve seam. Pin the sleeve in the armhole and check the fit. Reset the sleeves.

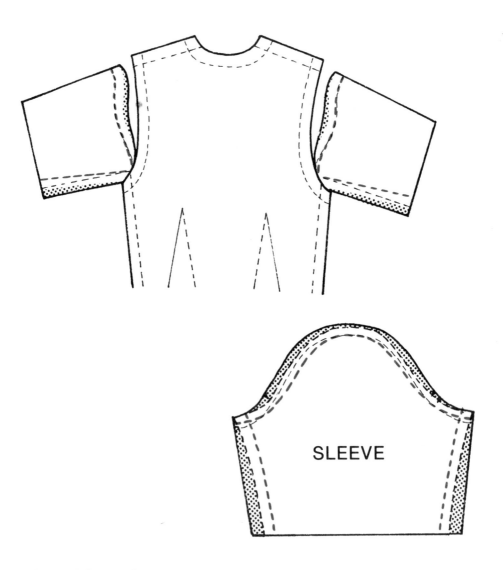

SLEEVE

The old stitching line is shown in black, the new stitching line is shown in red. Material to be trimmed off is shown by gray shading.

PATTERN SOLUTION   Slash the pattern from point A to point B and overlap the amount necessary to eliminate excess sleeve fullness. Tape the pattern in this new position. True the pattern edges if necessary.

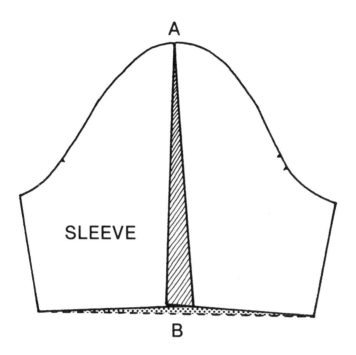

The area to be overlapped is shown by black lines. The area to be added is shown by gray shading.

SEWING SOLUTION   A raglan sleeve that droops unbecomingly is too big. Put the garment on inside out. Pin up the front and back shoulder seams an equal amount from point A to point B. Pin up the underarm seam, tapering to nothing where the sleeve meets the armhole. If the sleeve is still too full, pin up the long shoulder dart to eliminate excess fullness. If the sleeve is very full, you may want to continue this dart all the way down the center of the sleeve as a seam. Mark your corrections with tailors' chalk. Take off the garment and stitch up the darts, then the underarm seams, and, finally, the shoulder seams.

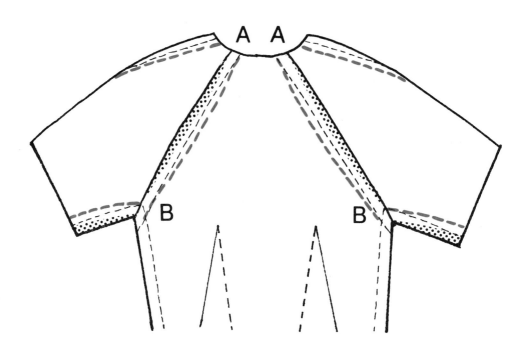

The old stitching line is shown in black, the new stitching line is shown in red. Material to be trimmed off is shown by gray shading.

PATTERN SOLUTION   Slash the pattern from point A to point B through the point of the dart. Overlap the amount of correction necessary and tape in new position. Redraw your dart, enlarging if necessary to take up extra fullness in the shoulder area. You may want to taper your dart, as shown, to avoid getting a point or bump at the end of your shoulder where the dart stops. True the pattern edges if necessary.

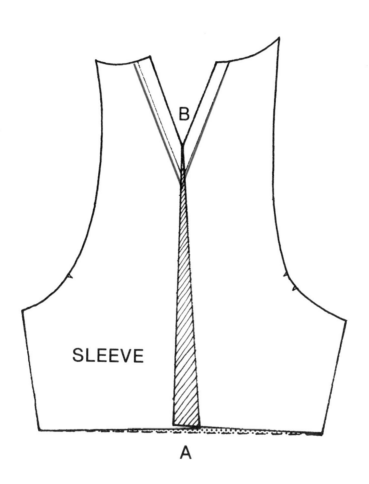

The area to be overlapped is shown by black lines, the area to be added is shown by gray shading. New dart lines are shown in red.

SEWING SOLUTION   A raglan sleeve that is too tight has horizontal pulls around the sleeve parallel with the sleeve edge. Let out the front and back seams an equal amount from point A to point B. Let out the underarm seam from point C to point D. Restitch the long shoulder dart in a convex shape as shown in the drawing and rip out the old stitching. These corrections should be sufficient to eliminate the wrinkles and allow more comfortable movement.

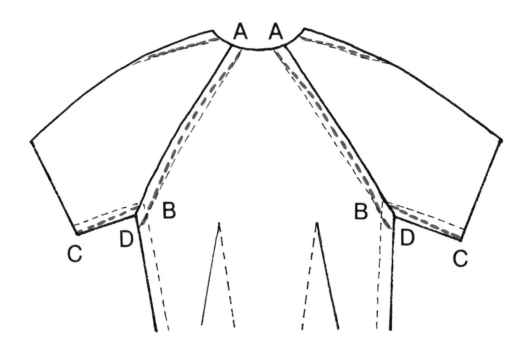

The old stitching lines are shown in black, the new stitching lines are shown in red.

PATTERN SOLUTION   Slash the pattern from point A to point B through the point of the dart. Spread the amount of correction necessary and tape in place over a piece of tissue paper. Redraw your dart in a convex shape to allow more shoulder room. True the pattern edges if necessary.

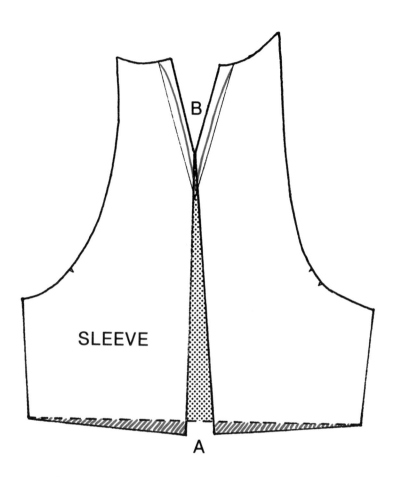

The area to be cut off is shown by red lines. The area to be added is shown by gray shading. New dart lines are shown in red.

SEWING SOLUTION   If you have narrow shoulders a raglan sleeve will droop and fall off the end of your shoulders. The best correction you can make on a finished garment is to simply shorten the point of the long shoulder dart as shown below, and restitch the dart. Rip out the old dart stitching. This correction gives the illusion of a better shoulder fit.

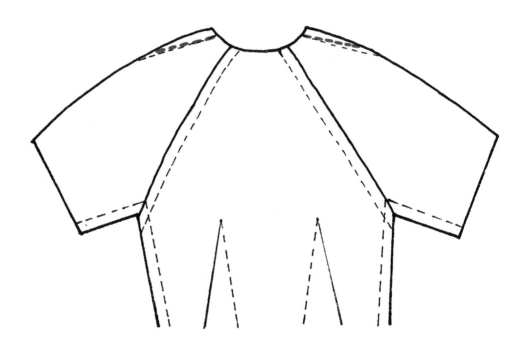

The old stitching lines are shown in black, the new stitching lines are shown in red.

PATTERN SOLUTION   Slash your pattern from point A to point B and overlap by the amount that the raglan sleeve falls from your shoulder. This has the effect of shortening the dart and eliminating excess shoulder fullness. Tape the pattern in this new position. True the pattern edges where necessary.

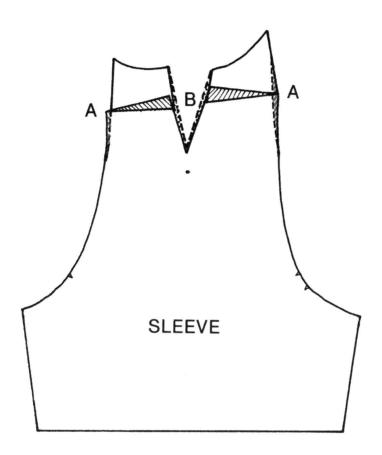

The area to be overlapped is shown by black lines, the area to be added is shown by gray shading. The area to be cut off is shown by red lines.

SEWING SOLUTION   Broad shoulders cause a raglan sleeve to pull uncomfortably. Let out the front and back seams an equal amount from point A to point B, tapering into the old stitching line at point B. Lengthen the point of the dart until it sits over the acromion, the knobby bone at the end of the shoulder. Restitch the dart in a convex shape as shown.

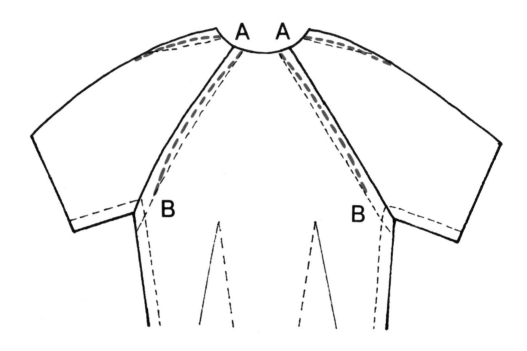

The old stitching lines are shown in black, the new stitching lines are shown in red.

PATTERN SOLUTION   Slash the pattern from point A to point B and spread the amount necessary to make the end of the dart sit over the acromion, the knobby bone at the end of the shoulder. Tape the pattern in this new position over a piece of tissue paper. Redraw the dart in a curved shape as shown.

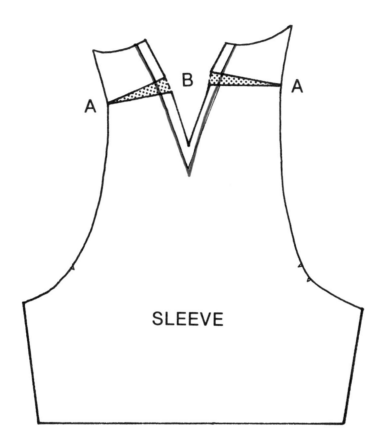

The area to be added is shown by gray shading. New dart lines are shown in red.

DRESSES

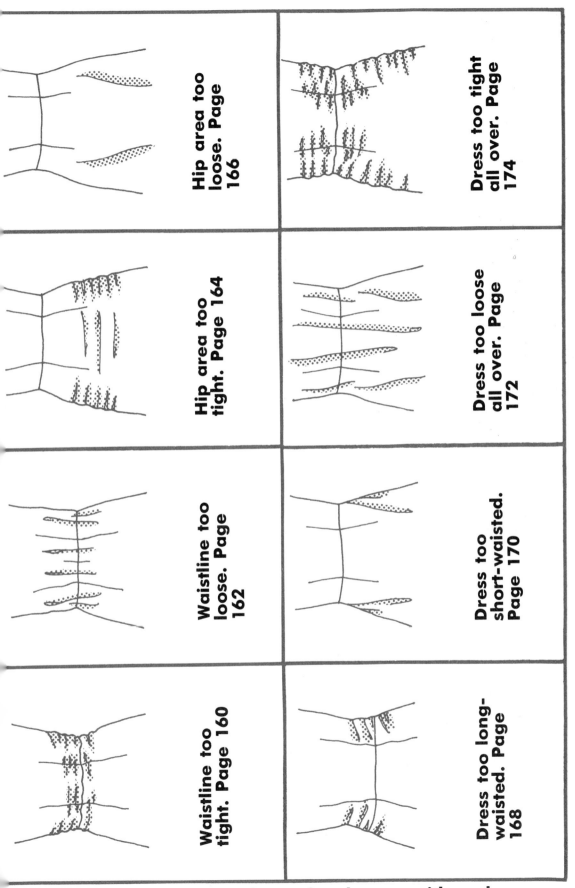

Hip area too
loose. Page
166

Dress too tight
all over. Page
174

Hip area too
tight. Page 164

Dress too loose
all over. Page
172

Waistline too
loose. Page
162

Dress too
short-waisted.
Page 170

Waistline too
tight. Page 160

Dress too long-
waisted. Page
168

**All corrections will be shown for dresses with and
without a waistline seam.**

SEWING SOLUTION   Tight horizontal puckers around the waistline are an indication that the waist is too small. For a dress with a waistline seam, rip the seam all around up to about 1″ from either side of the zipper or closing. Rip the bodice and skirt darts both front and back and about 4″ of the bodice and skirt side seams. Put the garment on inside out. Pin up the darts and side seams to achieve a smooth fit, being sure to make an equal correction on the bodice and skirt so that the waistline seams will still match. Mark your corrections with tailors' chalk. Take off the garment and resew the darts, side seams, and waistline seam. For a dress without a waistline seam, rip the darts and rip the side seams from points A to B. Put the garment on inside out. Pin up the darts and side seam, letting out enough to eliminate the puckers. Mark the corrections with tailors' chalk. Take off the garment and restitch the darts and side seams.

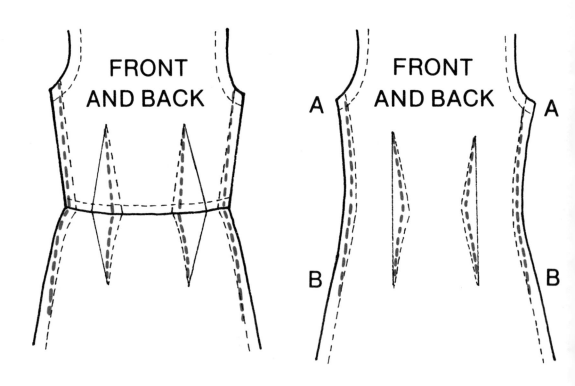

The old stitching line is shown in black, the new stitching line is shown in red.

PATTERN SOLUTION   For a dress with a waistline seam, determine how much you need to add to the pattern to eliminate puckers, and add this amount to the bodice at point A and to the skirt at point C. Connect point A with point B as shown, and point C with point D, blending into the hip curve. Make your darts smaller. Make these corrections both front and back, dividing your correction between these areas to keep the pattern balanced. Make an equal correction on both bodice and skirt to keep the waistline seams the same size. For a dress without a waistline seam, add to the waistline from points A to B, both front and back. Make your darts smaller.

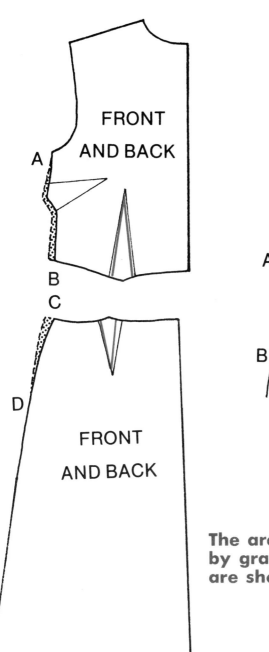
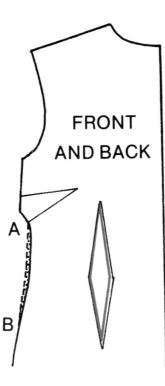

The area to be added is shown by gray shading. New dart lines are shown in red.

SEWING SOLUTION   Vertical droops in the waistline area mean that the waist is too big. For a dress with a waistline seam, rip the seam all around up to about 1″ from either side of the zipper or closing. Put the garment on inside out. Pin up the darts and side seams until you have eliminated the excess fabric, being sure to make equal corrections on the bodice and skirt so that the waistline seams will still match. Mark your corrections with tailors' chalk. Take off the garment and resew the darts, side seams, and waistline seam. For a dress without a waistline seam, put the garment on inside out. Pin up the side seams and front and back darts until you have eliminated the excess fabric. Mark your corrections with tailors' chalk. Take off the garment and restitch the darts and side seams.

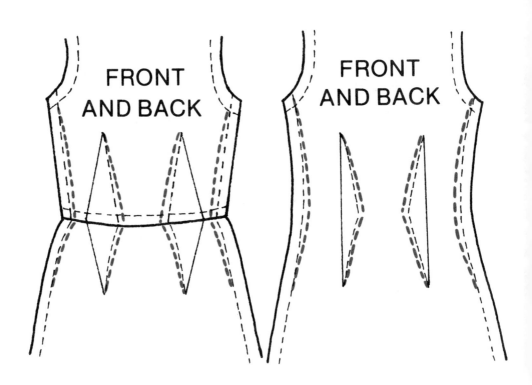

The old stitching line is shown in black, the new stitching line is shown in red.

PATTERN SOLUTION   For a dress with a waistline seam, determine how much you need to take off the pattern to get a smooth fit. Mark this amount point A on the bodice, and point C on the skirt. Connect point A to point B, and point C to point D, blending into the hip curve as shown. Make your darts larger. Make these corrections both front and back, dividing your correction to keep the pattern balanced. Make an equal correction on both bodice and skirt to keep the waistline seams the same size. For a dress without a waistline seam, pare the waistline down the necessary amount between points A and B, both front and back. Make your darts larger.

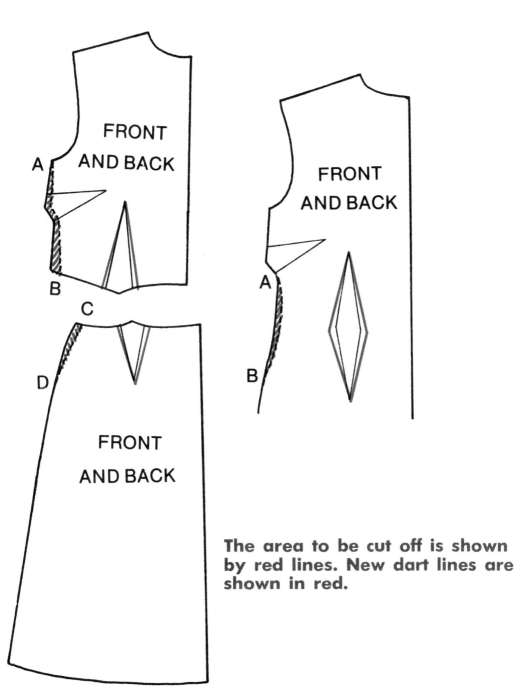

FRONT AND BACK

FRONT AND BACK

FRONT AND BACK

The area to be cut off is shown by red lines. New dart lines are shown in red.

SEWING SOLUTION   Horizontal puckers across the hips mean the dress is too tight there. The correction is similar for dresses with or without a waistline seam. Let out the side seams as much as possible from point A to point B. If the garment has a center front or center back seam, let it out from point C to point D. If the dress is very tight, these corrections may not completely eliminate your problem. If the puckers are in the upper hip area, sewing your darts in a convex shape, as shown below, may help.

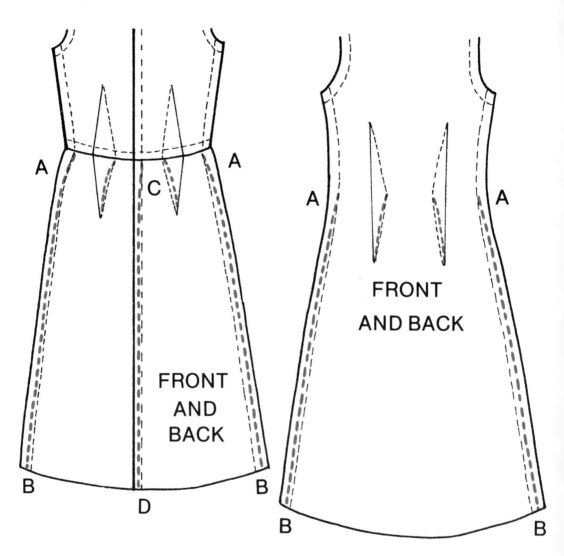

The old stitching line is shown in black, the new stitching line is shown in red.

PATTERN SOLUTION   The correction is the same for dresses with or
without a waistline seam. Using your fashion curve, add to the side seams an
equal amount from point A to point B. Add enough so that the skirt will hang
smoothly over the curve of your hips without wrinkles. The dotted line is your
new cutting line.

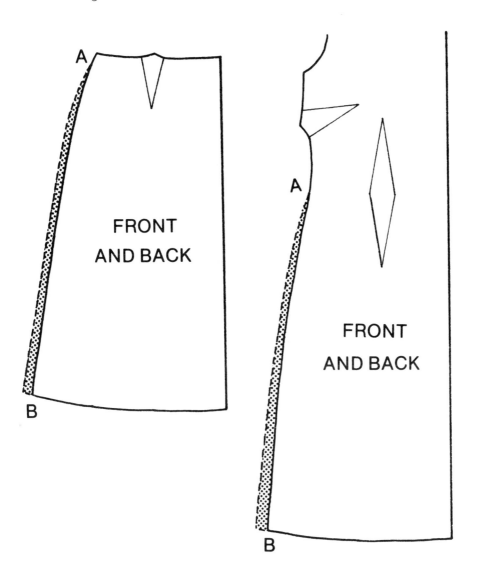

**The area to be added is shown
by gray shading.**

SEWING SOLUTION   Vertical droops over the hips through the length of the skirt mean that the hip area of the dress is too big. The correction is the same for dresses with or without a waistline seam. Put the garment on inside out. Pin up the side seams as much as you need to eliminate extra fullness. Mark your corrections with tailors' chalk. Take off the garment and restitch, sewing in a smooth even line from point A to point B. Trim off the excess seam allowance.

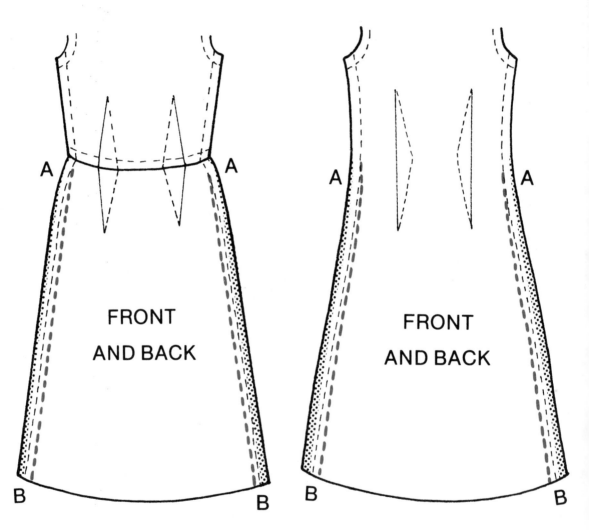

A

A

FRONT

AND BACK

B

B

A

A

FRONT

AND BACK

B

B

The old stitching line is shown in black, the new stitching line is shown in red. Material to be trimmed off is shown by gray shading.

PATTERN SOLUTION   The correction is the same for dresses with or without a waistline seam. Pare the hip area down an equal amount, front and back, from point A to point B. Use your fashion curve to maintain a natural-looking hip curve. You should take off enough to make the skirt hang smoothly without puckering. The dotted line is your new cutting line.

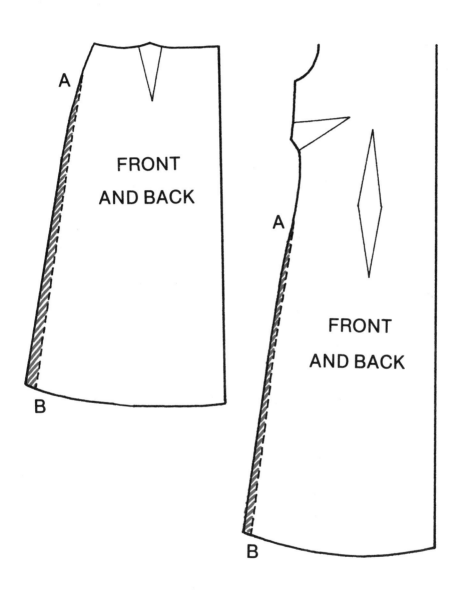

The area to be cut off is shown by red lines.

SEWING SOLUTION   A dress that is too long-waisted will have horizontal folds of extra cloth above the waistline seam, and tight horizontal pulls below the waistline seam where the hip curve begins. You will get similar problems even on a dress without a waistline seam when the waist is cut too low for your figure. For a dress with a waistline seam, rip the seam all around to the zipper or closing. Rip the zipper from the skirt section. Put the two pieces of the garment on inside out. Pin the skirt in the correct waistline position and mark the correction with tailors' chalk. Take off the garment. Restitch the waistline seam and trim off the excess seam allowance from the bodice. Reset the zipper. For a dress without a waistline seam, restitch the side seams as shown below. This has the effect of shortening the waistline. If the darts have not been clipped too far, restitch them as shown, moving the central points of the darts up toward the natural waistline.

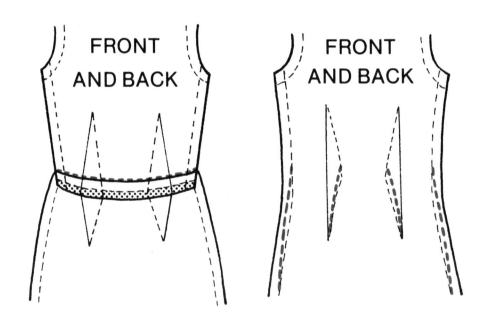

The old stitching lines are shown in black, the new stitching lines are shown in red. Material to be trimmed off is shown by gray shading.

PATTERN SOLUTION   For a garment with a waistline seam, slash the front and back bodice patterns from point A to point B and overlap the amount necessary to put the waistline seam in the correct position. True the side seams and redraw the darts. For a dress without a waistline seam, determine where your natural waistline is and mark this on your pattern. Using your fashion curve, start drawing the hipline curve immediately under the waistline and blend into the existing pattern edge. Make the same correction both front and back. Raise the center points of the darts to the natural waistline as shown below.

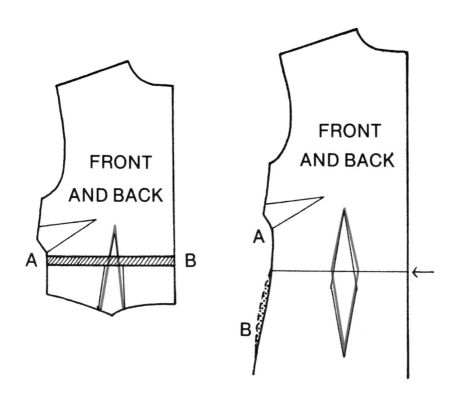

The area to be overlapped is shown by black lines, the area to be added is shown by gray shading. New dart lines are shown in red.

SEWING SOLUTION   A dress that is too short-waisted will fall in vertical sags from the natural waistline through the hips. For a dress with a waistline seam, rip the zipper from the skirt section up to about 1″ above the waistline seam. Resew the waistline seam, letting out as much as you can. If you do not have enough material in the waistline seam to make the correction, you may insert a piece of matching cloth and simply wear a belt or scarf over the seam. Reset the zipper. For a dress without a waistline seam, restitch the side seams as shown below. Resew the darts, moving the central points of the darts down toward the natural waistline. Trim the excess from the side seams.

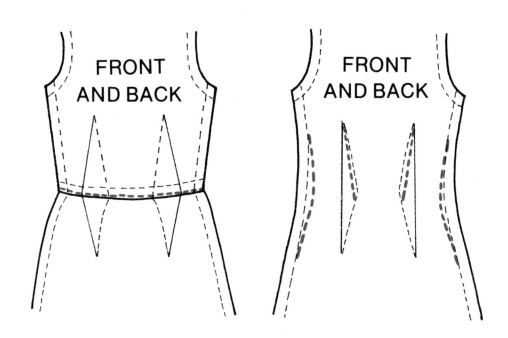

The old stitching lines are shown in black, the new stitching lines are shown in red.

PATTERN SOLUTION   For a dress with a waistline seam, slash the front and back bodice patterns from point A to point B and spread the amount necessary to put the waistline seam in the correct position. True the side seams and redraw the darts. For a dress without a waistline seam, determine where your natural waistline is and mark this on the pattern. Draw the waistline down to this mark and blend into the hip curve as shown. Make the same correction both front and back. Lower the center points of the darts to the natural waistline as shown below.

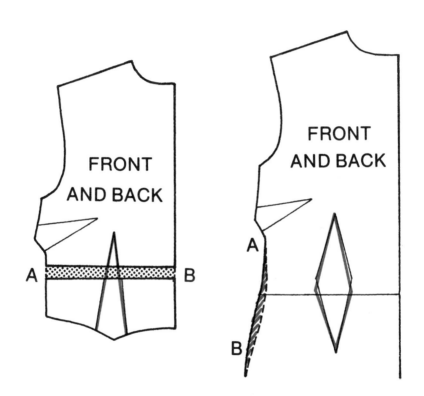

The area to be cut off is shown by red lines, the area to be added is shown by gray shading. New dart lines are shown in red.

SEWING SOLUTION   A dress that falls in loose vertical sags is simply too big all over. For a garment with a waistline seam, rip the waist all around up to about 1″ from either side of the zipper or closing. Put the garment on inside out. Pin up the side seams and darts until you are satisfied you have a smooth fit. Make sure that you pin up equal amounts on the bodice and the skirt so that the waistline seams will still fit together. Mark your corrections with tailors' chalk. Take off the garment and restitch the darts, the side seams, and the waistline seam. For a dress without a waistline seam, put the garment on inside out and pin up the side seams and darts until you get a smooth fit. Mark the corrections with tailors' chalk. Take off the garment and resew the darts and side seams. Trim off the excess seam allowance after making corrections.

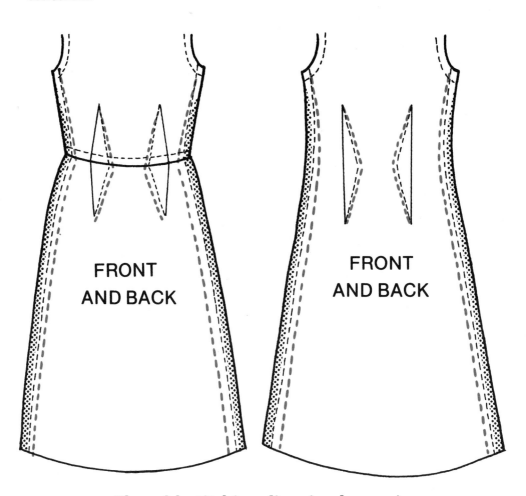

FRONT AND BACK

FRONT AND BACK

The old stitching line is shown in black, the new stitching line is shown in red. Material to be trimmed off is shown by gray shading.

PATTERN SOLUTION   For a dress with a waistline seam, pare an equal amount (whatever you determine is necessary) from the bodice and skirt patterns between points A and B, and points C and D. Use your fashion curve to redraw the hipline. Make your darts larger. For a dress without a waistline seam, pare down the pattern equally, front and back, between points A and B. Make the darts larger.

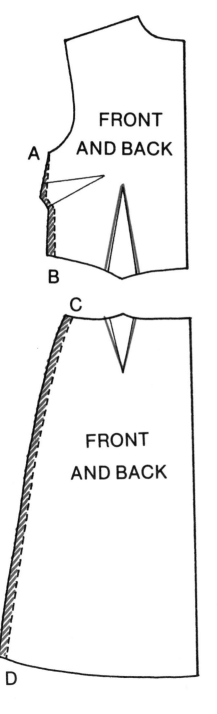

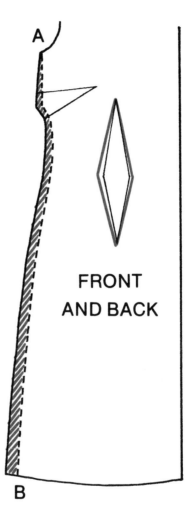

The area to be cut off is shown by red lines. New dart lines are shown in red.

SEWING SOLUTION   A dress that has tight pulls all over is too tight. For a dress with a waistline seam, rip the seam all around, up to about l″ from either side of the zipper or closing. Let out the side seams as much as possible between points A and B, and points C and D. Let out the darts as much as necessary; if you need a lot of extra room you may want to let them out completely. Restitch the waistline seam. For a dress without a waistline seam, let out the side seams as much as possible between points A and B. Let out the darts as needed; you may let them out completely if necessary. *Please note:* If the dress is extremely tight, all these corrections may still not give you enough room to correct the problem.

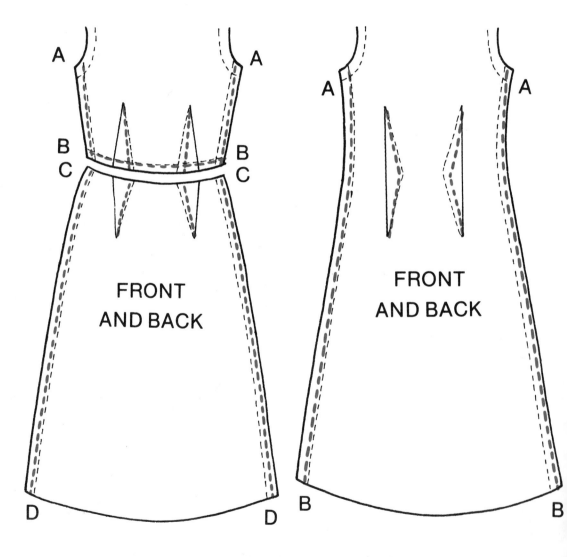

The old stitching lines are shown in black, the new stitching lines are shown in red.

PATTERN SOLUTION   For a dress with a waistline seam, add an equal amount (whatever you determine is necessary) to the bodice and skirt patterns between points A and B, and points C and D. Use your fashion curve to redraw the hipline. Make your darts smaller. For a dress without a waistline seam, add to the pattern equally, front and back between points A and B. Make the darts smaller.

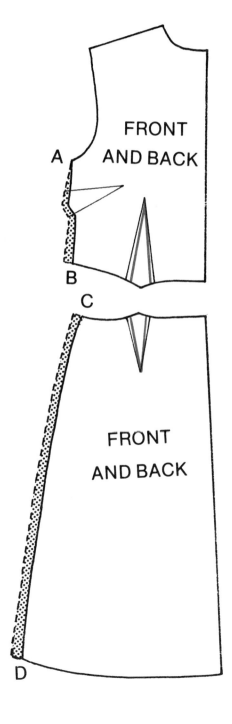

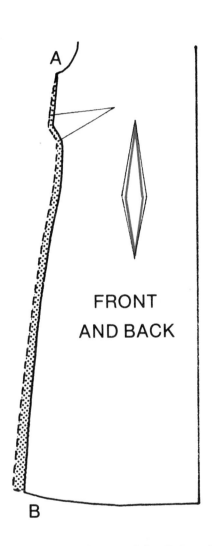

The area to be added is shown by gray shading. New dart lines are shown in red.

Index
of
Fitting
Problems

Problem	Sewing Solution	Pattern Solution

Pants

Skirts

Bodice